A ROUGH KNIGHT FOR THE QUEEN

A ROUGH KNIGHT FOR THE QUEEN

PHILIP JOSÉ FARMER

EDITED BY PAUL SPITERI

Meteor House

A Rough Knight for the Queen
by Philip José Farmer

Meteor House
ISBN 978-1-945427-18-3
First Paperback Trade Edition

With thanks to Craig Kimber, who owned the only copy of this manuscript and could have kept it to himself, but graciously chose to share it with the world.

Meteor House would like to dedicate this book to the memory of Scott Turk. Husband, friend, wit, and scholar. But, above all else, a damn fine man. Losing him is like losing a piece of our collective soul.

Sir Richard Francis Burton
The Erudite Adventurer

Despite his life and achievements being both historically verifiable and wholly grounded in a very real world, Sir Richard Francis Burton might seem to have been a character straight out of a fantasy novel. He wasn't. He was one of the greatest heroes of Victorian society, at a time when the explorer was held in the kind of awe which today is reserved for top footballers or pop stars.

But can we seriously imagine, say, a David Beckham representing Her Britannic Majesty's government as a consul on four different continents? Or travelling across the post-bellum United States to discuss polygamy with the leader of a dynamic religious sect? Or translating Renaissance Portuguese poetry into English? Can we picture a Robbie Williams as a master swordsman (*Brevet de Pointe*), a reporter from a war zone which killed over 50% of the local population (Paraguay), or the inventor of a new type of military carbine? No? Well, Burton did all these things and more, much more.

"Fantasy" did, however, play a role in Burton's life, not least in his well-documented habit of encouraging and even telling exaggerated stories which reflected badly on himself, perhaps in a Sufi-esque attempt to invite opprobrium and thereby test his own strength of character, or in his translations of *One Thousand and One Nights* with its tales of jinn, rocs, mystical journeys and "The Lady with Two Coyntes."

In his original writing, too, Burton did not eschew fantasy, of which the following are clear examples.

His poem *Stone Talk* takes the form of a conversation between the drunken Dr. Polyglot (surely Burton himself) and a flagstone in London's Fleet Street, in which they discuss and criticise the mores of contemporary society and many of its leading figures. Such an idea really does come from the world of fantasy, although Burton's wife, Isabel, did not think so, in that she bought up as many copies of the initial print run as she could to prevent it from coming to the attention of the objects of her husband's acerbic observations which she feared would have damaged his career.

Isabel's attitude towards Burton's other extended poem, the mystical *Kasîdah*, was the exact opposite, despite it being a further example of her husband's involvement with fantasy, and certainly did not reflect her own devout Catholicism. Burton first developed the idea of *The Kasîdah*—a philosophical discussion between representatives of different faiths—Hindu, Frank (that is, Christian), Muslim, Buddhist, Sufi/Soofi, Theist—during his pilgrimage to Mecca in 1853, and he continued to revise and expand the poem until its eventual publication in 1880. However, rather than giving his own name to a work which was obviously very personal ("*Do what thy manhood bids thee do, From none but self expect applause; He noblest lives and noblest dies, who makes and keeps his self-made laws.*"), Burton not only hid his authorship behind the fantasy name of Hâjî Abdû El Yezdî,[1] but he also claimed the original had been translated into English (from an unspecified language) by "F.B.," a certain "Frank Baker," that is, Burton's second name Francis plus his mother's maiden name, Baker, in Vienna, the capital of the then Austro-Hungarian Empire where Burton was serving as British consul in its major port, Trieste. This "Frank Baker" also wrote "biographical notes" about the "author," with the description that included: "*To a natural facility, a knack of language learning, he added a store of desultory reading . . . . Nor was he ignorant of the -ologies. Briefly, he*

---

[1] Spelling and punctuation vary but this format will be used throughout as it mirrors Burton's own usage.
Also note, Sir Richard's original spellings for place names appear through the book.

had every talent save that of using his talents." This being, of course, not biographical but an autobiographical summary of Burton's own characteristics. This was fantasy within fantasy, a fictitious author "translated" by a *nom de plume*.

When Isabel re-published *The Kasîdah* in her *The Life of Captain Sir Richard Francis Burton*—giving full credit to her husband as the sole, original author—she included only the poem itself and ignored the initial quotations from Shelley and St. Augustine (strange bedfellows indeed), the introduction "To the reader," the thirty-seven pages of notes—such notes being a hallmark of all of Burton's writing—and the conclusion he wrote and which should all be considered integral parts of the overall work.

My third example of Burton spinning a web of fantasy is the case of "The Kama Shastra Society of London and Benares" with its printing shop in Cosmopoli. This "society" was pure fantasy, as it existed only in the mind of Sir Richard Burton (and that of his friend and collaborator, Forster Fitzgerald Arbuthnot) and as mere words on the page, but it served as an essential vehicle for publishing Burton's erotic translations *The Kama Sutra, The Ananga Ranga,* and *The Perfumed Garden* to avoid the attention of the National Vigilance Society and almost certain prosecution for obscenity. So successful was this deception, this fantasy, in the 1880s, that the (in this case genuine) translators did indeed escape prosecution. And even well into the 20th century, pirated editions of these books often tried to prove their erotic credentials by claiming to be published by, for example, the "Kama Shastra Society of Cosmopoli London, Benares and New York," some seventy years after Burton's death!

The best (or worst) example of fantasy in Sir Richard Burton's original writing—rather than his translations—is his identifying a Sotadic Zone, within which "*The Vice* (that is pederasty—not to be confused with paedophilia) *is popular and endemic, held at worst to be a mere peccadillo . . .*" Burton gave a meticulous description of the so-called geographical extension of the "zone" specifying that it was "*bounded westwards by the northern shores of the Mediterranean (N. Lat. 43 °) . . . (narrowed to embrace) Asia Minor, Mesopotamia and Chaldæa, Afghanistan, Sind, the Punjab and Kashmir . . . (before broadening) to enfold China, Japan and Turkistan . . ."* and so on. This treatise was originally published as a codicil to *The Book of a Thousand Nights and a Night*, although nowadays it is more often printed as a standalone book. This "study" of the occurrence of and an explanation for male homosexuality—which carefully avoided including the United Kingdom within this Sotadic Zone—seems laughable today, but it should be remembered that was probably the first attempt to explain the phenomenon of homosexuality in a non-judgemental way, and this several years before Oscar Wilde was vilified, essentially tortured through "hard labor" and driven into exile.

Given what can surely be described as Sir Richard Burton's "fantastic" life, if not a life of fantasy, it should come as no surprise that he attracted the attention of a modern fantasy writer like Philip José Farmer—himself no stranger to the use of a *nom de plume* (Kilgore Trout, "author" of *Venus on the Half-Shell*)—who not only included Burton as a major character in his Riverworld series, but also wrote the biography you are about to read.

Michael Walton
(Author of *Sir Richard Francis Burton and his Circle*)

Philip José Farmer
The Liminal Writer

As I imagine is the case for many people, I first encountered Sir Richard Francis Burton in Philip José Farmer's *To Your Scattered Bodies Go*. I was fifteen at the time, and this remarkable character so captivated me that I immediately purchased a Burton biography. It wasn't one of the better ones, as it turned out, but it was enough to get me collecting and reading his works, along with everything else that had been written about him. I feel I came to know him pretty well over the ensuing years; sufficiently, at least, that I can confidently assert that he was driven—as I am, and as I'm pretty sure Phil was—by a lifelong fascination with all things liminal.

"Liminal" refers to that threshold state wherein a person, thing, or situation is in the midst of transition, passing from one state into another, but not there yet. In esoteric rituals, it refers to the exact moment when consciousness begins to alter; where the shaman becomes aware that he is detaching from this world but is not yet immersed in the vision he has summoned.

In the *I-Ching*, liminality is represented by Hexagram 20: Kuan. In form, the Hexagram resembles a gate, and in meaning it suggests "the act of passing through" where both sides are visible but the observer is neither completely on one nor completely on the other.

This notion of being permanently poised between two conditions, situations, or environments was, I think, at the core of Burton's being. Having spent his childhood being hauled back and forth across Europe by his incurably restless parents, never fully belonging anywhere, he entered Oxford University as a Britisher who didn't know how to be British. The manners and mores of his supposed homeland were alien to him. He emulated them, but emulation is a sham, and to those for whom the social customs came naturally, the sham was transparent. Their nickname for him, "Ruffian Dick," only underscored his inability to pass fully through the gateway and become one of them. No wonder he turned to other cultures.

Much is made of Burton's talent for disguise, for blending in with Indian and Arabian natives. Disguise, though, is just another pretence, and reading between the lines, one gets the sense that he was, to some extent, humored by those with whom he mingled. There's a degree of braggadocio in his accounts, as if he were informing his countrymen that, though he wasn't accepted by them, he had no problem being accepted by others. However, you only need glance at the remarkably copious footnotes in his works to see that Burton was incapable of being anything other than singular, an outsider, an observer, always watching, always analysing, never assimilated.

Of course, there's another way to cross a border. If you can't get through the gate, you can bypass it; you can transgress. Burton was fascinated by transgressions, and as an inhabitant of the uptight Victorian era, transgressive sexual practices were an obvious target for his unceasing curiosity. Sex is one of the most basic of human behaviors, so when he wrote extensively about sexual activities that were considered unacceptable in one culture but were regarded as perfectly normal in another, he was, in fact, making a broader point, highlighting the absolute hypocrisy of all the standards by which his countrymen had judged him.

All of this made him the ideal protagonist for *To Your Scattered Bodies Go*. A river is a natural boundary. How appropriate, then, to have him travel along (rather than across) the seemingly endless one on Riverworld!

Boundaries and transgressions are the hallmark of Phil Farmer's fiction. Where Riverworld explores a horizontal partition, the

World of Tiers offers a series of vertical ones. In *The Lovers*, *Strange Relations*, *Image of the Beast*, and *Blown*, sexual barriers are explored and defied. Then we have Phil's enthusiasm for Tarzan (manifested in Lord Grandrith and Lord Tyger), a man who, just like Burton, exists at the junction between the uncouth and the civilized. On Tarzan's flip-side, there's Doc Savage (or Doc Caliban), whose knowledge, physique and behaviour were all "programmed" into him by his father—an aggressive act of "civilizing"—yet he's Savage by name and "savage" by nature, in that he employs all of that acquired behavior in violent physical confrontations with criminals.

The themes that pervaded Burton's life and Phil's fiction have always resonated with me, which is why I also chose Burton as a protagonist. In my six "Burton & Swinburne" novels, the boundary is time, the liminal moment the transition from one sequence of consequences into another, parallel set. My version of the man is constantly questioning his position and role in history. Maybe the real Burton felt the same way, an individual trapped in the wrong period, possibly better suited to the 20th and 21st centuries, into which Phil and I brought him, than he was to his native 19th.

In the end, though, despite my attempts to keep him travelling through history, and Phil's to have him traverse the length rather than the width of the river, the gateway 'twixt life and death was one that Burton passed through without hindrance. What remains, a mass of literature, regrettably few photographs, tells us a lot but by no means everything. The true nature of Sir Richard Francis Burton remains a complex, alluring, and frustrating mystery.

Mark Hodder
(Author of the Burton & Swinburne series)

BURTON AND FARMER
INCREDIBLE ADVENTURES AND ETERNAL WRITINGS

"Enjoy thy shining hour of sun;
we dance along Death's icy brink,
But is the dance less full of fun?"
— The Kasîdah of Hâjî Abdû El Yezdî

Before anything else, I would like to record my gratitude to Mick Walton and Mark Hodder for their compelling and profound introductions to this quite rare work by Philip José Farmer. I certainly don't think we could have asked for more. And as they say, after the Lord Mayor's show . . .

Sir Richard Francis Burton and Philip José Farmer are crossing points on the same web. You pass through one to get to the other. But the link—the gate—works both ways as, for many people, an appreciation of Burton comes via Farmer.

Mick's insight into Burton, complemented so well by Mark's piece on Farmer, brings out the best in both of these heroes. I will not pretend to be able to emulate their words, concepts, and insights but I will try and give you some history behind *A Rough Knight for the Queen*, and give my own view on why I think Farmer and Burton are essentially two sides of the same coin. They may never have met but they are forged from the same ore. Phil never explored Africa or the Amazonian forests of Brazil but he shared Burton's lust for adventure and he exercised this yearning via his writing. As much as Burton may have felt he was born out of time (what an Elizabethan he would have made!) so Phil, to my mind, would have excelled and thrived in the formative years of his country's history. And on these shoulders of giants we have people such as Mick and Mark, among so many more.

But let me write a little about the history of this piece.

"A Rough Knight for the Queen" was written in 1953, originally for a men's magazine (Phil claims it was called *Gonads*—I can picture the curl at the edges of his mouth as he says this) but it was not published until decades later. Phil considered expanding the piece into a full biography of Burton but when Fawn Brodie's book was published in 1967, Phil felt he didn't have anything additional to add so the manuscript was filed away. Many years later still, knowing that he would never revisit the project, Phil sold the manuscript. Only a small handful of fans were even aware of the biography's existence and when work started on a volume of rare Farmer works, permission was given for "A Rough Knight for the Queen" to be included.

That volume became *Pearls from Peoria*. Although not published until 2006 by Subterranean Press, the road to publication was bumpy and circuitous, as book projects can often be. A year or two before it was ready to sit on bookshelves, as part of my editing duties, I'd decided that each piece in the book should have a short introduction explaining its provenance. I also wanted to share any interesting nuggets of information with the reader. To that end I ventured to Peoria, Illinois to meet up with Phil. I wrapped a family holiday to the Midwest around the meeting but was able to spend most of one day with the Farmers in their wonderful and inviting home. While my good friend, Tracy Knight, and I talked with Phil in his study, my wife, daughters, and Sharon Knight spent time being entertained by Bette Farmer. We covered a lot of ground that day, getting input from Phil on the content of the book. Minutes later (at least it *felt* like minutes) we were dragged out to rejoin the rest of the group. In that time we covered a myriad of subjects far beyond the contents of *Pearls*, but every syllable, every thought, every second, was precious. Now, years later, I still have that essence of how great that conversation was even if I can't recall every sentence as I once could.

To be fair, only a fraction of that time was spent talking about "A Rough Knight for the Queen," but I do remember the shine in Phil's eyes when we alighted on the subject of Burton. It wasn't a look of nostalgia, or idolatry, it was a gaze of deep respect, empathy, and understanding. That Burton was a hero to Phil is an understatement. And not just a physical hero. We know Phil respected the adventures and explorations that Burton made during his life, but Phil also had a deep appreciation of Burton's writings and personal philosophy. Of course this includes Burton's interest in Sufism but it was also much more. Burton was bigger than the sum of his parts. He was an eminent linguist, a hyperpolyglot, a fearless explorer, a famed Arabophile, a poet, a writer, a translator. And I could go on: cartographer, diplomat, spy, ethnologist, sexologist, swordsman. More? Soldier, devoted husband, and philosopher. Any person, with just three, four, or even five, of these accomplishments would be a person of stature and be rightly lionized.

But Burton valued knowledge above everything else. He once wrote of a library he wished he could have had: ". . . and I'd like to think that I could read those books forever and forever, and die unlamented, unknown, unsung, unhonored—and packed with information."

(Does this remind you of anyone?)

Even with all these traits and values hewn into a man of bone and sinew, Burton was more. Something you can't quite place your finger on—the interspatial element that binds it all together and adds mass—the man-god particle, if you will. Elusive but undoubtedly there.

In the 1860s Burton spent time in Santos, Brazil. While there he started translations of the great 16th Century Portuguese poet-explorer Luís de Camões, a man with whom Burton felt a deep sense of kinship. Over the next twenty years Burton continued to work on these translations as well as his own "commentary" of Camões and his greatest work, *The Lusiads*. These works eventually saw publication while Burton was resident in Trieste towards the end of his illustrious life.

During his time in Trieste, Burton also published his own epic poem, *The Kasîdah of Hâjî Abdû El Yezdî* ("Hâjî Abdû El Yezdî" being Burton's alias, as Mick Walton has already pointed out in his introduction). It's no great leap to see that working on *The Lusiads* for all those years paved the way for *The Kasîdah*; one influenced by the other. Farmer himself noted that *The Kasîdah* was itself a spark for the Riverworld series.

Camôes to Burton, Burton to Farmer, Walton, and Hodder. Life is a trickle-down. Life is a rich tapestry of connections. That magical web.

For my own part, it was reading the Riverworld series that brought the real Burton to life (again, and again). On Riverworld everyone who has ever lived is suddenly reborn along the banks of a planet-girdling river. Their basic need for food is provided daily for them but this does not stop humanity reverting to type and exhibiting its usual inhumanity. Phil's incredible concept gave him free reign to make protagonists of anyone in history and explore the philosophical and physical conundrum of why, and by whom, they had been given a second chance at life. In fact, more than just a second chance as no-one who dies on Riverworld stays dead for longer than a day. Perhaps one lifetime just isn't enough for enlightenment to be achieved, to complete that path that Sufism espouses as its adherents strive to obtain direct experience of God.

Burton was no longer that paragraph or two in a childhood history book; he was now the larger-than-life adventurer and explorer that we, this readership, know he was. A man who took enormous risks, not out of disregard of his own life, but because it was the only way to source the knowledge he craved; to get to the *truth*. Like Percy Fawcett (another explorer who perhaps lived after his time, and coincidentally, like Burton, was born in Torquay), he was driven by an inner conviction to learn more, to *discover*. As an aside, some may be interested to know that Fawcett was an inspiration for Conan Doyle's Professor Challenger, as well as Indiana Jones, and, potentially, The Shadow.

Knowing of Farmer's knowledge and respect for Burton, it is no surprise that the explorer is one of the main protagonists of the Riverworld saga. In his introduction to *River of Eternity* Phil talks about how he originally used the name "Black" as a pseudonym for Burton because he wasn't sure if he was permitted to use real historical names (I won't go into the whole story here but *River of Eternity* is an early draft of *To Your Scattered Bodies Go*—alas, not the *original* draft!). I sometimes wonder if Phil ever deliberated using the name Frank Baker. (As Mick Walton noted in his introduction, a nom-de-plume fashioned from Burton's middle name and his mother's maiden name.)

Phil's knowledge of Sufism grew over the years, mostly from an intellectual standpoint, but in the late 1970s Phil wrote (of the first draft of his Riverworld novel): "It's not easy now to separate my own philosophy and Burton's in the writing of the original novel. I may have directly used some of *The Kasîdah*'s concepts and attitudes of mind. Or I may just have found some of my own concepts and attitudes reinforced when I read the poem."

It is in *To Your Scattered Bodies Go* that Sufism emerges in Phil's writing but it certainly didn't end there. *The Unreasoning Mask*—assuredly one of Phil's most accomplished novels—chronicles the quest of Captain Ramstan, would-be savior of the pluriverse, as he struggles with his lapsed Sufi faith.

In *Escape from Loki*, one of the young Doc Savage's referenced mentors is the fictional Hâjî Abdû El Yezdî, narrator of Sir Richard's *The Kasîdah*.

And many years after writing about Burton and Sufism in the early Riverworld stories, Phil revisited the faith in one of his final stories, "Coda" (1993). A touching and poignant tale, told in the first person, it details the path Alfred Jarry, the late nineteenth century French dramatist, takes under the tutelage of Rabi'a al-Basri, the famed eighth century sufi and teacher. This is a very personal story suffused with Phil's own meditations and with a referenced cameo by Burton.

Farmer felt a kinship with Burton on many levels. Farmer was the master at creating heroes and bringing them to life, but in Burton he found a ready made hero. However there is a note of lamentation in Farmer's words. Phil speculates on what

Burton would have been able to accomplish if he had received the inheritance that was meant for him. How his life would have been different and easier. It's hard not to imagine that Phil also shared those feelings. Although the figures are drastically different, Phil was swindled out of a significant sum he was due for winning a writing competition. That money would have given Phil a level of independence that would have allowed him to focus more fully on his writing instead of having to rely on employment to support his family. We can only speculate and bewail what stories and adventures we have missed out on, and what extra adventures Phil may have been able to include here if Burton had received his just bequest.

Phil and Sir Richard may never meet on the river-planet but I'm sure they would be fast friends if they ever were to. And who should doubt that they would explore that world, and enjoy adventures neither could have experienced or written of before.

Vive, valeque!

Paul Spiteri

Postscript

There are many wonderful resources out there for anyone wishing to know more about Burton or Farmer. As well as the books they each wrote (and what better way to get an understanding of a man than from his own writings), there are three websites I would like to suggest.

The magnificent Burtoniana.org is an exceptional repository of photographs, works, and information on Burton.

For all things Farmer related please visit the Official Philip José Farmer website, pjfarmer.com, and the International Bibliography, philipjosefarmer.com.

Sir Richard Francis Burton circa 1854. Photograph possibly taken in Aden. A relaxed pose but there's no mistaking the determination in the eyes.

Philip José Farmer, aged 35, photo taken in Philadelphia after he won the Hugo award as most promising new talent.

Please note that this book was originally written at a time with less regard to sensibilities that we take for granted now. And, indeed, the work itself refers back to characters and events from an even less enlightened, colonial, time. It should not be inferred that the author supported any of the views being expressed, nor events being described. In fact, we knew Philip José Farmer to be a sensitive, liberal thinker with attitudes way ahead of his time. As publishers of *A Rough Knight for the Queen*, Meteor House has taken appropriate and prudent steps to moderate the language used without affecting the understanding or intent of the story. It goes without saying that Meteor House does not endorse or support the portrayal of any negative stereotypes.

A ROUGH KNIGHT FOR THE QUEEN

Storms were always blowing up in Richard Burton's path and changing or frustrating his plans. Sometimes, the storms were raised by mediocre men who blew hot in their jealous efforts to thwart him. Other times, Nature did her best to trip him up. She it was who was now stalling Burton's expedition into East Africa to search for the unknown headwaters of the Nile. And it was men who would put the finishing touch to that old bitch Mother Nature's interference.

Richard Francis Burton, captain in the Bombay Army of the East India Company, landed at Berberah on April 7, 1855. Berberah was located on the northern shore of the east horn of Africa, on the Gulf of Aden. Burton had just come back from Aden, situated across the Gulf in southwest Arabia. Only a short time before, he had plunged into the Ethiopian wilderness with a few natives and had become the first European to visit the forbidden city of Harar. Thirty explorers had tried to enter its walls and had died; he alone had met and had outbluffed the all-powerful and murderous Amir of Harar. Now, he and three English lieutenants were to set out from Berberah, would revisit Harar, and then go into the jungle to find the source of the Nile.

Everything went well at first, ominously so. Fifty-six camels were purchased, and a small army of mercenaries, armed with sabers and flintlock muskets, were hired. Instead of starting at once, the unfortunate decision was taken to wait for the mid-April mail from England, which was to contain surveying and navigating instruments. But on the ninth of April, the monsoons began with a storm. The next day the city of Berberah was almost deserted, for the Bedawin preferred to travel in the rainy season,

31

when they could find water easily. Eleven days later a gunboat from Aden landed a dozen Somali who wanted to go with Burton as far as Ogadayn. Though Burton asked the boat to stay, it left. However, a native ship anchored, and though it meant to leave that same evening, Burton, fortunately, ordered a rice and date feast for the crew and captain. They decided to stay over.

At sundown, Burton inspected the camp. As he strode about, swaggering, he made an impressive figure. He was a broad muscular man about six feet tall with jetblack hair and eyes. He carried himself proudly and moved abruptly, like a startled panther. His eyes were unusual, described by friends and enemies alike as being piercing, stinging, hypnotic, unfriendly, savage. He sported a dragoon's thick moustache, and his jaw looked hard and strong enough to bite an iron bar in two. He radiated strength and authority, so that any visiting native would have had no trouble in picking out the leader from the four white men.

All seemed to be well. The camp had been pitched on a rocky ridge close to a creek, about three-quarters of a mile from the city. Lt. Stroyan's tent was on the extreme right, Lt. Speke's on the left, and in the middle was the *rowtie*, a sepoy's tent, supported by two uprights and a transverse and open at both ends. Burton and Lt. Herne slept there. The horses and mules were tethered in the rear, and the camels in the front. At night, two sentries were posted, and these were kept from sleeping by regular visits from the native and English officers.

Suddenly, shots were heard from behind the tents. Burton raced to find the cause of the commotion and was told by the guards that they had fired over the heads of three horsemen. They were afraid that these were the scouts of a raiding party, and they'd tried, and failed, to scare them off.

Sharply, Burton said, "From now on, don't do any bloody shooting unless you know it's absolutely necessary. And then don't shoot over them. Shoot their bloody heads off!"

After giving this characteristic order, he questioned the three Bedawin. They replied that the local sheik of the Abban tribe was in a neighboring port with four ships. He intended to occupy

Berberah when it was deserted and build a fort there. The three had come to see if the ship in the harbor carried building materials. Laughingly, they asked if Burton feared danger from them. All believed their story and went to bed without any uneasiness.

Sometime between two and three in the morning, the Balyuz, the native commander, ran into the tent, shouting that the enemy was on them. Burton leaped out of bed and listened for just a second. The rush of men outside sounded like a stormy wind; it was evident that they were outnumbered. He called for his saber and ordered Herne to find out just how many the attackers were. Then, with a Colt in one hand, Herne ran to the rear and left of camp, where the most noise seemed to be. He looked for the mercenaries and found a few. The others had leaped from bed and run off into the darkness, not even waiting to pick up their weapons. Herne fired twice into the assailants, without being able to see if he'd struck anybody. Finding himself alone, he ran back to the tent. Something hard struck his legs and sent him sprawling on the ground. The tent's pegrope. As he started to rise, a Somali leaped from the darkness, his warclub lifted. Lt. Herne fired, and the man crumpled. When he burst into Burton's tent again, he found Speke also there, for the captain had aroused him. Stroyan was nowhere to be seen. Speke had been awakened by the musket fire, but he thought it was the normal false alarm, warning thieves away, and tried to go back to sleep. Then, hearing clubs beating on the sides of his tent and the shuffle of naked feet, he ran into Burton's tent.

The Somali, three hundred and fifty strong, attacked the three Englishmen and the Balyuz, the only native who had not run away. They swarmed outside the tent, trying to nerve themselves with fierce screams. Javelins flew into the opening of the tent, and long heavy daggers were cast at the occupants' legs. Burton, armed only with his saber, ordered Herne to his right and Speke to his left. Each had one pistol, which they fired until their ammunition was gone. So close were the spearsmen, a man fell at every shot. Herne rose to search for his powder horn in the rear of the tent. "Damn, I can't find it," he called out. Then, "There's usually some spears tied to the centerpole." He ran back to Burton. "One of them is slashing through the rear of our tent. They'll be on our backs in a moment."

Just as he ran out, the tent sagged, for its ropes had been cut in the hope that the English *Roumi* would be caught within, where they could be stabbed like fish in a net. Burton, knowing this trick, had ordered them out. He led them straight into the whole mob. Just outside the entrance were about twenty Somali, kneeling and crouching behind their shields, their spears held out before them. They looked like black-faced ghosts, with their ostrich feathers atop their bleached yellow-white hair, and their white robes edged with scarlet.

Burton rushed into the twenty, his saber swinging. Clubs swung at him and seemingly bounced off his hard muscles or else were turned aside by the steel blade. He smashed through canvas-covered shields, then, unexpectedly, drove the point into their throats. These savages had never heard of thrusting with a sword; they were dead before they had caught on. And many of them suddenly found their spears and clubs had dropped out of useless hands. Burton used the *manchette*, a trick of swordplay which had helped earn him the title of *maître d'armes* from the French. A cut at the forearm, then an unexpected backhand drawing, the sharpened backedge of the saber slicing the nerves and tendons of the enemy's wrist.

Speke and Herne were swallowed in the horde. Burton was left alone. Thinking that he saw Stroyan's body lying on the sand, he cut his way towards it. Meanwhile, the Balyuz, who could not use his spear because of a sore right thumb, was trying to help Burton out. His efforts were limited to pushing him along. Burton, thinking he was an enemy, turned to cut him down.

"For the sake of Allah, it is I, your friend!" cried the Balyuz.

Burton halted the sword at the top of his swing. Instantly, a Somali who had been lurking at the edge of the fight for just such a chance, stepped forward and drove his broadheaded spear through Burton's cheeks. Then he turned and fled, escaping the avenging cut at him.

Though the blade had knocked out four of his back teeth and

driven into his palate, Burton fought on, the spear hanging from the side of his face. The savages, though wild to gain the glory of killing this great warrior and of soaking their ostrich crests in his blood, could not stand before his fury. Within a minute he was in the darkness, where some of his mercenaries and servants offered to go back with him. But as he approached the enemy once again, they faded off into the night, leaving him alone. Meanwhile, the Balyuz reappeared. Burton ordered him to go to the native boat in the harbor and tell it to wait for them. The rest of the time before dawn he spent in wandering about looking for his three companions, the spear still sticking through both cheeks. Finally, his pain and fatigue were so great that he had to lie down.

At dawn he rose, and went to the head of the creek, where an armed party from the boat found him and carried him to safety. Fate, that so often had and would cast events to trip him up, had this time saved him, for had the boat left the night before, as they intended, he would have been slaughtered by the Somali in the daylight.

Stroyan's badly mutilated corpse was later found. Except for some bruises from warclubs, Herne was uninjured. Speke was captured and stabbed many times in the chest and thigh, but he escaped.

It would have been better for Burton if Speke had died there, for it was the lieutenant who was to rob Burton, on a second expedition, of the glory of having discovered the Nile headwaters, after Burton had borne the burden of the safari and fallen sick. Later he spread lies about the whole incident at Berberah, making it out that he, Speke, was the leader, was the first to turn out, and only he had the courage to defend himself. Moreover, Burton, instead of getting credit for the exploration into East Africa and a commendation for his magnificent fight at Berberah, was actually rebuked by the government, as if it had been his fault, and was also made a scapegoat for international political complications which arose from the incident. Burton had broad shoulders, but there were times when they would sag a little under the many misrepresentations and malicious lies made against him. Some of this persecution was his own fault, however, due to a total lack of tact and a brutal outspokenness. However mean and ornery his enemies, Ruffian Dick, as he was sometimes called, was meaner and ornerier.

Almost from the first, Richard Burton showed his famous streak of contrariness and self-contradiction. Born in Barham House,[1] England, on March 19, 1821, he was a beautiful blue-eyed and redheaded baby of distinguished ancestors. One of them was Louis XIV, the Sun King of France, who had had a bastard son by the beautiful Countess de Montmorency. From them he probably got his black hair and eyes. Another famous ancestor was Rob Roy, the Scottish outlaw. From him he probably got his red hair and blue eyes. He did not, of course, get both sets of colors at the same time. He was born with the light coloring, and his maternal grandfather, old Mr. Baker, was so overjoyed that he decided to will to little Richard his fortune of 80,000 pounds. That is good money today, and was worth more than six times as much in those days. Apparently, redheaded Richard had been born with a silver spoon in his mouth.

But his mother, the very person who might have been thought to have guarded this windfall for her first child, was the very one who cheated her son out of it. She had a passionate attachment to her wastrel half-brother, in whose favor the will had originally been made out. For three years she argued with her father against changing the will. Finally, the old man said that it was his money, and he'd do what he wanted to with it. He drove in a carriage to his lawyers to carry out the change. And dropped dead of a heart attack at the door. Richard's uncle got the money, was at once swindled out of 60,000 pounds in Paris, and later lost it all.

Meanwhile, Richard's red hair and blue eyes, as if to demonstrate his contrariness and to show that he was captain of his own body, if not of his grandfather's money, changed to a jet black. And so they remained the rest of his life.

Afterwards, his childhood was spent in being dragged over

---

[1] Richard Francis Burton in his autobiography erroneously (or, perhaps, deliberately) claimed he was born at Barham House. He was, in fact, born in Torquay, Devon.

France and Italy while his hypochondriac father searched for relief for his asthma. His mother, not to be outdone by her husband, also developed her professional illness. The boys had a succession of drunken and brutal tutors and of governesses who could not keep them in hand. Mr. Burton, a retired Lt. Colonel on half-pay, took up boar hunting and developed the unfortunate habit of riding head on into trees. Many times he was brought home unconscious, leading the neighbors to think he was dead drunk. Richard and his brother and sister grew up rather wild. Very early his talents for exploring, his daredevilry, his love of swordsmanship and fast women, his facility with languages, and his quick temper, began to show. At three he began to learn Latin; at four, Greek.

In Sorrento, Italy, there was a great natural arch which the peasants told him could not be climbed. He and his brother did so, anyway, though the crumbling stone and great height made it very dangerous. And when Mt. Vesuvius erupted, the boys ran across a lava stream in smoking boots and dared the Italians to follow them. No one did. There were many deep vents which gave off poisonous gases; at the Grotto Del Cane a dog was lowered in a basket half a dozen times a day for visitors to watch its asphyxiation. Burton had himself lowered, and was pulled up just in time to keep from being completely overcome. Meanwhile, Col. Burton was making their houses chokingly unbearable with his stinking experiments at soapmaking. Burton and his brother Edward became drunk for the first time and visited a cathouse, though only as sightseers, being too young for anything else. Burton broke his violin over his teacher's head, which effectively ended his forced lessons. At Naples, the cholera plague struck. The dead were hauled away at nights in carts. They were dumped into huge pits above which hung a blue flame; gases lit from the festering bodies piled below. Dick and Edward stole out at night, masked like the deathwatch, and helped load the corpses. Neither caught the plague, and it was during this time that both became interested in medicine. Later, Edward became a doctor, and Dick was always very good at amateur doctoring, both for animals and men.

At a very early age Burton took fencing lessons from Cavalli, the most famous rapiersman of the time. Even then he began his idea of combining the best points of the French and Italian schools into one system. Meanwhile, the two boys disdained masks until the day Dick drove his foil into Edward's uvula, almost destroying it.

Burton's early days were spent in just such pranks, all calculated to relieve his boredom and drive his parents frantic. His father, however, persisted in his desire that both his boys go into the Church, so he sent them to Oxford with that idea in his mind. Not theirs, for Edward speedily managed to annoy the dons until they "rusticated" him, or, in plain words, kicked him out. Richard took a little longer. He became very interested in the Near East and decided to learn Arabic and Hindustani. Unable to find a teacher who knew much of either subject, he began to teach himself Arabic and soon perfected a system whereby he could learn a language in two months. It was then that he met Don Pascual de Gayangos y Acre, a Spanish Arabist. This fellow burst into laughter when he saw Richard's self-taught method of writing Arabic letters, for they were written from left to right, that is, the wrong way. But he admired Richard's daring and ability in tackling such an obstacle by himself.

Burton soon came to the conclusion that he cared neither to become a minister nor teacher. Bored with college, he began easing himself out. He played a hundred students' pranks. Once he had himself lowered by a rope into the garden of an old don, and there removed many of the choicest flowers by the roots and replanted huge marigolds in their place. He liked to shoot birds with an air gun as they flew over the heads of the teachers out playing lawn bowls. The dons would pick up the birds and theorize as to how they died, only to find out when blood dripped on their clean clothes.

He gambled, being unusually lucky at public game houses though not so much at private card parties, got drunk, drove tandems (forbidden to the students), went on a visit to Heidelberg, where he and his brother scared hell out of the roistering, swaggering, bragging German saber-dueling students. Unmasked, the two gave a display of their skill and then challenged any comers. They got no takers. Finally, Richard deliberately went to a horse race when he was supposed to be at a lecture. Summoned before the college dignitaries, he boldly though unsuccessfully defended himself, and the next day Richard drove off in a tandem over the flower beds of the dons, kissing his hand to all the pretty shopgirls he knew—and he knew too many of them for his own good. He left college forever.

The Afghan War was raging, and Richard thought he'd like to get in it; there was a good chance for rapid promotion during wartime when soldiering for the East India Company. The officers died like flies, though more from disease than bullets. Too poor to afford the Guards or other crack regiments, he bought a commission in the Bombay Army, and set out for India on the *John Knox*. The skipper, a tall Scotsman, wished to establish his reputation as a hard man to deal with and by way of doing so he challenged the young recruit with the black and burning eyes to a boxing match. Burton tore like a young Dempsey into him, beat him backward around the ring, punched him in the middle until he was sucking wind for breath, then knocked him down for good. Afterwards, he practiced upon the flageolet until his passengers and crew were driven crazy by the horrible squeaking, but nobody dared take this handy fellow with his fists to task. Finally, Burton found three Hindustani servants and set them to teaching him the language, much to the relief of everybody.

Full of eagerness, Burton landed at Bombay, only to find that the war was over. It would not be the last time that he arrived upon a scene of action just a bit too late.

Now that the chance for rapid promotion was over, there was only one way to rise in John Company's[2] service. That was through the slower and harder way of languages. Skilled interpreters were in demand, so Burton set himself to studying twelve hours a day, and in the seven years he served in India became a master of Hindustani, Gujarati, Persian, Maharati, Sindi, Punjabi, Arabic, Telugu, Pushtu, and also learned Turkish and Armenian. His first

---

[2] The informal name for the East India Company.

teacher told him that he was a man who could learn a language running, and he was later given the Brahminical thread by the Hindu wise men, an honor few people got. Burton noticed that the *Bibi* or white woman was rare at that time in India and that most of the officers solaced themselves with a *Bubu*, a native woman. He was not above living with some of these "walking dictionaries" as he called them; besides providing him with the comforts a man needs at home or away, the *Bubu* was an easy way to learning a language and the customs. She kept house for him, managed the servants and the money, nursed him when sick, and had a neverfailing recipe for preventing motherhood, if the man so desired.

Tired for a while of living with either man or woman, Burton set up a household with forty monkeys. He taught them to eat from plates while servants waited on them and he talked to them. He claimed that he could converse with them and that he had compiled a dictionary of sixty of their words. Unfortunately, the book was later lost in a fire.

There were other amusements. He learned the fine art of falconry from a Baloch chief and mastered it so well that they accused him of being a Muslim. He wrote a book on it, *Falconry in the Valley of the Indus*, which is still a fine work consulted by those who want to learn something of the native art.

He had a horror of snakes. To overcome it, he took lessons from snake charmers, so well that he soon was petting cobras.

At Karachi in the Sind, Burton and his friends used to visit a pool of sacred crocodiles. While the keeper was kept occupied with a bottle of cognac, they blasphemed the sacred beasts by teasing them. One fellow skipped across the pond by leaping from one scaly back to another. Burton, using a chicken for bait, hooked a monster reptile. After landing it, he tied its jaws together with a rope, then leaped on its back and rode it as it raced towards the pool. When the swiftly running reptile was about to slide into the water again, he jumped into the air to one side, high enough to avoid a blow from its tail that would have broken every bone in his body.

About this time all his boyish playing came to an end. He met Captain Walter Scott, a nephew of the famous author of Ivanhoe. The captain was looking for a good man to help him in surveying the Sind canals for their possible improvement. As Burton was not only regimental interpreter but had taught himself the use of compass, theodolite, and level, Scott picked him. His duties were to wander over the districts, leveling the beds of canals and making preparatory sketches for a grand survey. Since he was thrown so much among natives, he came to depend upon them for society. He began a systematic study of them. To get to know them better he decided to pass himself off as one of them. After trying several disguises he settled on that of a half-Arab, half-Persian from the shores of the Persian Gulf. Thus he could explain his imperfect accent to the Sindi people. About this time his fellow officers, who did not understand why he should hang around the natives, began to call him "the white n———." Burton, as usual, on hearing of insults, laughed. He gloried in them, and, besides, no one would have called him that to his face. There were few if any swordsmen or pistol shots the caliber of Burton in all India.

One day a certain Mirza Abdullah of Bushiri, a *bazzazz* or seller of fine linens, calicos, and muslins, stepped out of a tent into which Sahib Burton had gone. Long hair fell to his shoulders, his beard was long, and his face, hands and feet were very brown—with henna. Only one who had known it was he could have detected Burton. This Mirza wandered over the countryside with a single native servant and seemed to spend more time talking than selling. Occasionally he would open a shop and sell figs, dates, tobacco, molasses, and strong-smelling sweetmeats. He was very popular, for besides being a good looking fellow, he liked to pass gossip around, could tell wonderful tales, and always gave the ladies, especially the good looking ones, heavy weights for their money. Added to all this was a repertoire of magical tricks. In no time at all everybody came to look forward to his visits, he was welcome at private homes, in the market, and the mosque. Sometimes he even gained entrance to a harem, and several times proud papas offered their daughters' hands to him.

He came through every experience unrecognized; this adventure was to prove the prelude to the far more important time when he would pose as a dervish and make the pilgrimage to the city of Mecca. As a matter of fact, the seven years he spent in India, though seemingly wasted at the time, were to prove wonderful tune-ups for his later, more famous trips to forbidden cities and lost lakes.

Some people think that it was upon Burton that Rudyard Kipling based his famous character of Strickland, the Englishman who could so successfully pass himself off as any of a dozen different kinds of natives. Burton's wife said that Strickland even talked like Burton.

Then came the Sikh War which was to add the Punjab to British possessions. A chance for glory again, and for swifter promotion. Burton, though a hardworking scholar, was essentially a man of action who thirsted to lead. He had trained his native troops as best he could in the use of the saber, teaching them to do more than slash; to cut and parry, to use the point, if need be. He marched with the 18th Bombay Regiment from Rohri on the 23rd of February. April 2nd, he was back, miserable and deflated and tired. The war was over.

Tempers were soured among the young officers who had been waiting for a chance at combat. Burton began making doggerel rhymes on men's names at mess, but knowing something of his commanding officer's touchiness, passed him over. The hot-tempered colonel, ordered him to write one on him. Burton, never one to resist a dare and also resenting the order, wrote:

"Here lieth the body of Colonel Corsellis;
The rest of the fellow, I fancy, in hell is."

The Sikh war might be over, but war with his C.O. was now officially declared. There was little Corsellis could do against him, but he would go disguised as a native and, riding a camel through the gates of Hyderabad, pass Corsellis, who never once knew his impertinent subaltern under the turban and beard.

Burton's adeptness at disguises got him into very bad trouble with the East India Company and the Foreign Office. Sir Charles Napier, the governor, wishing to know more of the native vice in the sinkholes of the cities of the Bind, asked Burton to investigate them. Burton joyfully accepted this very dangerous mission. If there had been the slightest suspicion at any time of his true identity, he would have died on the spot, for these bhang-smokers and homosexuals did not wish any white man to be nosing around them. So it was a tribute to his mastery of language and knowledge of custom that he came out alive. Of course, Burton overextended himself and surpassed his orders. As Frank Harris was to say of him many years later, "It was the abnormalities and not the divinities of men that fascinated him." So detailed and shocking was his report that it was hidden away in the files, presumably there never to see publication. But when a new administration entered, the papers came to light. The governor was hostile to any friend of his predecessor and when these papers, so offensive to the Victorian prudery of those days, were drawn to his attention, he put a black mark against Burton's name. It was totally unfair, this listing of him to be passed over for promotions and to be gotten rid of at the first excuse. It was almost as if they'd suspected Burton of having taken part in the perversions and orgies that he had witnessed. Some of the evil rubbed off on him, and he was never to get rid of it, in their eyes, at least.

An honest and dangerous job that would in another age or with another type of brass have gotten him a medal or a citation, had ruined his chances of success. Indeed, his very detailedness was praiseworthy, for Burton was the forerunner of the scientifically trained anthropologist of today; his books were to be used as reliable textbooks by a later generation of Ph.D.s. But his name was mud on John Company's list.

He was not permitted to take part in the Mooltan[3] campaign.

---

[3] The 1848 Mooltan Revolt and subsequent Siege of Mooltan began in April 1848 when local Sikhs murdered two emissaries of the British Raj. The Mooltan Revolt triggered the start of the Second Anglo-Sikh War and resulted in the fall of the Sikh Empire in 1849.

The interpreter's position was given to an officer who could only speak one native tongue, and that not nearly as well as Burton.

Stricken with a recurrence of a painful eye disease, almost blind, discouraged, thinking he was an utter failure, his seven years of hardships and constant study wasted, Burton applied for sick leave and left for Europe. Yet he had an understanding of India and an ability that should have made his superiors consider him as its viceroy. And he was on the verge of the greatest exploit of his life.

Burton was twenty-nine when he went to France in 1850. There he went through a typical rest cure for him, which consisted of furious practice with the rapier and saber. So good was he that he became one of the very few Englishmen awarded the *brevet de pointe* by the French, thus making him a *Maître d'armes*. He favored the *manchette*, which was a cut at the opponent's forearm, made in *tierce* or outside and vertically, followed by one in *quarte* or inside, horizontally. He developed the devilish trick of sharpening the false or dull back edge of his saber, so that when he withdrew the blade during a manchette, it would cut the nerves, perhaps the tendons, and cause his enemy's sword to drop.

During this time he began writing his *Complete Book of Bayonet Exercise*, intended for the British Army. Instead of being thanked for this valuable work, he was rebuked by his friend, Colonel Sykes. "Relying on the bayonet will make the men in the ranks unsteady," said Sykes. This was a time when every other army in the world except England's recognized the value of the bayonet in close fighting. Burton knew that the lack of it was the weak point in their military system. Later, the Crimean War demonstrated to the high command that the English soldier was very much in need of training with the bayonet. So Burton's pamphlet was taken out of the pigeon hole, its dust blown off, and a few modifications, not improvements, made to it. For this he got not one word of thanks or congratulations from the Commander-in-Chief. One day he received a huge letter from the Treasury, informing him that he could draw from it the immense sum of one shilling. This was all he was to get.

Burton laughed grimly and set out for the War Office. If they owed him a shilling, by God, he'd collect it. Even that was not easily done, however, for he ran into red tape that could not have been more tangled if he'd come to collect a million shillings. After some very hard arguing with a dozen clerks and visits to as many different offices, he drew the one shilling. And as he stepped out of the War Office, he saw a beggar with his hand out. At once, he gave it to the man.

"Lord love yer, sir."

"No," said Burton, "I don't expect him to do that. But I dare say you want a drink?" And he jauntily strode away. If the Empire could sneer at him, he could repay it in the same coin.

While still on sick leave Burton decided to carry out the project which first brought fame to him, if not fortune. He wished to study thoroughly the "inner life of the Muslim," and to make a pilgrimage to the holy city of Mecca, which was to the Mohammedan world what Rome is to the Roman Catholic. With this difference; that all roads lead to Rome, whereas infidels were strictly forbidden, on pain of torture and death, to visit Mecca.

Research showed Burton that he would not be the first European to penetrate the forbidden walls. Several Italian and English converts, beginning with Joseph Pitts[4] of Exeter in the seventeenth century, had gone into Mecca. The Swiss Burckhardt,[5] in 1814, had made a famous pilgrimage in native disguise. But he'd been too

---

[4] **Joseph Pitts** (1663–1735?) was an Englishman who was taken into slavery by Barbary pirates in Algiers, Algeria in 1678 at the age of fourteen or fifteen. During his time in captivity, Pitts went through three masters over the course of more than fifteen years, with whom he travelled to Cairo and Alexandria. In 1704 Pitts published *A True and Faithful Account of the Religion and Manners of the Mohammetans*. The book includes some of the first English descriptions of Islamic rituals. Converting to Islam while a slave, Pitts was the first Englishman to record the proceedings of the Haj. His narrative was the first description of Islam and the manners of Muslims written by a European.

[5] **Johann Ludwig Burckhardt** (1784 – 1817) was a Swiss traveller, geographer and orientalist best known for rediscovering the ruins of the ancient Nabataean city of Petra in Jordan.

nervous to take notes or make sketches. Whereas Richard proposed to take his usual detailed notes and make many sketches.

His first step was to apply to the Royal Geographic Society, asking that they back him. He would take three years leave and then fill out that huge white spot on the map, the Rub Al Khali desert in southeastern Arabia. The Society voted him funds, but the East India Company refused to give him more than a year, which was to be for the purpose of studying Arabic, wherever he found fit. Probably, they hoped the troublesome lieutenant would come to grief, but if he did, they weren't going to pay his survivors a pension.

The evening of April 3rd, 1853, two Bombay officers walked into a rundown London house. A little later, one of them, Captain Grindlay, walked out. With him was a longbearded Persian, one Mirza Abdullah of Bushiri. Both hopped into a cab, whose shades were drawn as it hurried to the train waiting to take them to Southampton. At the port, the captain, acting as the Persian's interpreter, led him to their cabin.

It was absolutely necessary that Burton adopt the disguise so far from his destination. If the mysterious grapevine of the Near East had had enough warning of Burton's disguise, he would undoubtedly have ended up with a knife in his ribs long before he got to Arabia.

As it was, the other Muslim passengers had no suspicions of his true identity, with the exception of one. Burton took the chance of practicing on them; there were a hundred things he had to perform exactly right. When Abdullah drank a glass of water, he could not carelessly toss it off. He clutched the tumbler as if it were the throat of a foe and called out, "In the name of Allah, the Compassionate, the Merciful!" Then he swallowed it all at once, and ended with a satisfied grunt. Before setting down the cup, he sighed, "Praise be to Allah!" an expression of thanks which meant much when said in the waterless desert. And when a friend said, "Pleasurably and in health," he must reply, "May Allah make it pleasant to thee!" Moreover, he could not drink while standing, unless it was water from the holy well of Zem Zem, water given in charity, or that which remained after Wuzu, the lesser rite of washing. And he must use his right hand when he stroked his beard or ate, leaving the left or unclean hand for ignoble duties.

As the days passed and the *S.S. Bengal* drew closer to Alexandria in Egypt, Burton became more and more the character he'd adopted. This throwing himself headlong into his role was one of the reasons for his success. Like all born actors, he was the identity he'd assumed. Circumcised at the age of thirty-two, the better to pass as a Muslim, he found himself now actually regarding the uncircumcised infidel dogs with contempt. His fierce eyes glared at them, and he avoided the company of all the *Roumi*, except for his interpreter's, of course.

But once while he was pressing his face against his prayer rug on deck, he looked up into the eyes of a Turk who was curious to see this devout Muslim. Burton paled a little under his henna-stained skin, for it was Turabi, a friend of his, and from Turabi's burst of laughter there was no doubt he recognized him. Frantically, Burton made signs to him not to give him away. The Turk, after keeping Burton in an awful suspense for a few minutes, turned and walked away, still grinning. Later, he and Turabi met in private, where Burton disclosed to him what he was going to do. The little Turk was not displeased, for he knew the Englishman would be making the pilgrimage devoutly enough, not with the intention of mocking Mohammed's faith. He advised Burton on several points.

At Alexandria he stayed with John Wingfield Larking,[6] in a little house to one side of the main villa. Here he hired a local wise man and got him to coach him in memorizing the Koran, and in the various forms of prayers. He decided to drop the Mirza, or Mister, and became Shaykh Abdullah, the dervish. A dervish was almost a licensed vagabond, he could go anywhere without questions being asked. And in an hour of danger he had only to act insane, and he could go untouched, for the East respected the mad as being the favorite sons of Allah, the "touched of God." Also, since he knew a little medicine, he set himself up as a *hakim* or doctor. When not studying, he visited the baths and the coffee-

---

[6] British consul in Egypt and Burton's friend.

houses, hung around the bazaars and shopped. His fame as a good doctor and a magician—for he brought along his bag of tricks—spread rapidly. In a short time, men and women were hammering on his door. Again, he had access to harems, though he was always careful while there to act as a holy man should. One old patriarch offered him his daughter's hand in marriage.

At last he felt that he must leave Alexandria and move on. To do so, he had to ask for a passport. After being pushed around by many minor officials and roundly cursed, he got it at the British consulate, where he used very broken English. He almost came to grief when a native police officer tried to run him off.

"*Ruh ya kalb*! (Go, O dog!)" said the official, swishing a whip of hippopotamus hide in his hands as if he intended to use it. Burton, fighting hard to control his famous temper, threw away the plea he had meant to give about them being true brothers of the Muslim faith and replied with a curse. Then he turned away slowly, fists clenched. If the officer had struck him, he would have gone down beneath the hard Burton fists, and he could not afford to ruin his chances in such a manner.

A few days later, he was sworn at again, this time by an English officer because he had brushed up against him in his filthy coat and dirty blue baggy trousers. This was while he was boarding the *Little Asthmatic*, a Nile steamer bound for Cairo. With all his possessions wrapped into a roll on his back, and fingering a rosary which was large enough to be used as a flail if he was caught in a brawl, the Shaykh went aboard. The canal was at its worst, with the water level very low. Instead of thirty hours, the boat took three days and nights to reach Cairo, and they grounded four or five times every day. As an impoverished dervish, he'd taken third class deck passage. A roasting sun cut through the canvas awning as if it hadn't been there. At night cold dews settled on him like a Scotch fog. The ship's cook was the world's worst, and he could not touch the better food of the infidels. With the rest of the natives, he drank muddy water drawn out of the canal in a bucket, and he munched his bread and garlic. A group of French housepainters going to paint the Pasha's palace at Shoobra offered him a drink of strong wine. He thirsted, for though he preferred whiskey, he would have been glad of any alcoholic drink at that time to help pass the boredom of the voyage. Sadly, he had to turn it down, because his role as a holy man demanded he not touch the drink forbidden by the Prophet. He sat and smoked and spent most of his time fingering his rosary or else stared at the one pretty woman on board, a Spanish girl, and cursed inwardly again because she would be even more forbidden than the alcohol.

He met two destined to play big parts in his stay at Cairo. One, Miyan Khudabakhsh Namdar, was a short fat man who appeared too late to catch the steamer, yet would not give up because he would have lost his fare. For a long time he ran alongside the canal, stumbling, calling, praying, cursing, falling into hollows, puffing as he clambered uphill, stopping now and then to turn back and hurry his donkey-boy, who was carrying his carpet bag. Finally, the captain, after laughing himself sick, stopped the boat. A few minutes later Khudabakhsh, exhausted, lay down and slept on the deck. When he woke up, he introduced himself to the false Abdullah. He'd been a shawl merchant in London and Paris. Attracted to Burton's style of conversation, he invited him to stay at his house at Bulak. And though Burton disliked the fat overdressed fellow with his Indian manner of fawning and frowning at the same time, he accepted.

The other, Haji Wali, was to become a good friend.

At Bulak he found that the caravanserais were full, so he was forced to stay with the shawl merchant for ten days. The man became rather tiresome, because he was so full of Western ways of acting. But Burton's time was not, he thought, wasted. Not long after he had met him, the merchant whispered to him that the native troops in India, the Sepoys, were plotting a great uprising. Burton had no chance then to warn the authorities, but he was to do so later. And of course, as usual, he was ignored and his reports pigeonholed. If the War Office had paid same attention to him, heeded the warnings of a man who knew India, and had followed his advice, the bloody revolt of the Sepoys, the Black Hole of Calcutta, and the equally bloody and vicious reprisals of the

British might all have been avoided. But Burton was always to play the role of a bearded Cassandra to the Empire.

In Cairo, Burton found lodgings so scarce that he was forced to take a room in the Jemaliyah, the dirty brawling Greek quarter. In one way this was fortunate, for he ran again into Haji Wali. Together, they smoked the forbidden and highly intoxicating weed, hashish. Burton told him who he really was. Wali had been born in Russia, had traveled a great deal, and had discarded most of the superstitions and prejudices of the Muslims. "I believe in Allah and his Prophet, and nothing else," he said. He advised Burton to throw away the dervish's gown, large blue pantaloons, and short shirt.

"Get rid of everything that connects you with Persia. If you insist on being an *Ajemi*, you will get into trouble. In Egypt you will be cursed, in Arabia you will be beaten as a heretic, you'll pay three times what other travelers do, and if you fall sick you will die by the roadside, while those who would otherwise help you will spit on you."

Burton considered. It was true. The Persians belonged to the Shia sect. They had rejected the first three caliphs who had succeeded Mohammed as spiritual heads of the Muslims after his death. They claimed that Ali, the Prophet's son-in-law, was the rightful claimant, and they did not acknowledge the Sunna orthodox theory and practice. They added five extra words to the prayer and did other heretical thing that made the Sunni Arabs despise them.

So Burton became a Pathan, born in India of Afghan parents. To spread his reputation as a doctor, he began by treating the porter of the place where he stayed. This fellow, like most poor Egyptians, had a disease of the eyes. Burton poured silver nitrate into them, meanwhile announcing loudly that he never took a fee from the poor. Naturally, after the porter's eyes improved, he spread the good word. The poor flocked around, talked of this great and generous doctor, and soon the rich began drifting his way. Burton did not care whether he was paid or not. This was just as well, because there was no word for gratitude in any Oriental language that he knew. The natives would kiss your hand as long as they were sick. Cured, they would have nothing to do with you, especially when it came to paying the bill. But his reputation spread. Though he used some Western medicines, he also took advantage of the Eastern. The natives liked the huge bread pills, dipped in a solution of cinnamon water, flavored with asafoetida, and they enjoyed painful remedies, such as rubbing themselves with a horse brush until they were scarred.

Burton would administer the medicine with his own hand saying, "In the name of Allah, the compassionate, the merciful." After the patient had choked down the huge pills, Burton would intone, "Praise be to Allah, the curer, the healer."

He had fun playing the doctor. He would have liked to use hypnotism in his practice, for he was a pioneer in this, as he was in other things. But Wali advised against it, saying that it would detract from his reputation as a holy man. People would noise it abroad that he was using demons, and he would soon find the better class of patients steering clear of him. Burton took his advice; the Haji then built up Burton's reputation by praising him wherever he went. Across the way lived an Arab slave dealer, whose Ethiopian slaves were always sick. Burton cured half a dozen girls of the price-lowering habit of snoring. The grateful trader spread Burton's fame and talked of his devoutness.

Pilgrims wanting to go to Mecca began gathering around Burton. He hired two servants, Nur, a thieving East Indian youth, and Mohammed. The latter was from Mecca, was fat, humorous, loved women and wine at too early an age, and was too curious to suit his master. He'd known Englishmen in India, and this made Burton fear his disguise would be penetrated. He did buy from Mohammed his *kafan* or shroud, which every pilgrim takes with him to be buried in if he should fall by the roadside.

Others were Omar, a chubby Circassian youth who had run away from home; Saad the Devil, a giant slave sent by Omar's parents to bring him home. These, with many more, waited for Shaykh Abdullah to make up his mind to start, but he was having too much fun to wish to start the dangerous trip at once.

Then, one afternoon, a burly Albanian captain of irregulars swaggered into Burton's rooms. After a few choice insults, he grabbed a pistol from the doctor's bag. Burton, his black eyes blazing, and itching with a desire to blow off some steam collected during the fasts of Ramazam, snatched the pistol back. Fortunately, the mustachioed Albanian had forgotten to bring along his pistol, otherwise he would have gone for his own pistol, and Burton would have had a charge of murder on his hands—and possible exposure.

He glared into Burton's eye, trying to make the other drop his. But of all men, he had chosen the least likely. Every man who met Burton and wrote of him mentioned his eyes. Stinging, like a sullen serpent's. Compelling, hypnotic. Wild. Fierce. A caged leopard's. Burton's face revealed "a tremendous animalism, an air of repressed ferocity, . . ."[7]

The captain received the full impact of those eyes and dropped his own. His head whirling, he stumbled out. But in a few hours he was back to find out what kind of man this supposedly quiet Indian doctor was.

"By Allah, thou art stalwart for a *hakim* and a shaykh!" he bellowed. "Wrestle with me so that we may see who is the better man." He was bigger than Burton, but the Englishman never refused a dare. He grappled with the captain, and they stood upright, breathing garlic and wine in each other's faces, straining to upset the other. Everywhere Burton had gone, he had taken pains to learn the local secrets of self-defense, and now he used his strength, kept in shape by exercise with foil and boxing gloves, to aid his wrestling lore. He shifted his weight suddenly and followed it with a cross-buttock that sent the Albanian flying to the floor. For a minute the captain lay there, half-stunned. Then he jumped up, bellowing, not with rage but with delight. "By Allah, you are the kind of *hakim* I love! Let's have a drink on your victory, and another to our eternal friendship!"

---

7 ". . . a tremendous animalism, an air of repressed ferocity, a devilish fascination." ". . . his terrible magnetic eyes–the sullen eyes of a stinging serpent." Arthur William Symons (1865-1945). British poet and critic.
"He reminded me by turns of a black leopard, caged but unforgiving... eyes like a wild beast." Wilfred Scawen Blunt (1840-1922). English writer, poet, and explorer.

Burton knew better than to touch the forbidden alcohol, but the terrible demands of the Ramazam, the Muslim Lent, had left him drier than a camel's hoof. When the captain came staggering into the room, his arms burdened with bottles of the fiery *araki*, Burton did not refuse him. The stuff burned his veins and loosened his brain; soon he and the captain were singing songs and telling dirty jokes. One thing led to another; finally, the Albanian insisted they go out to look for some pretty girls to help them celebrate. They roared into the next room, where Haji Wali was trying to take a siesta. When he threw up his hands in horror at the idea of alcohol, they poured his slippers full of *araki*. And they charged out after the girls, only to stagger into a room kept by two old women. Scandalized, the sharp-tongued harpies scolded them so viciously that Burton became half sobered and dragged the captain home to his bed.

Next morning, the scandal was all over Cairo. The devout hakim's reputation was badly bent, if not broken.

Haji Wali, grinning, said, "You had better start on your pilgrimage at once."

Burton agreed, and took leave of his friends. But he was cautious enough to tell them that he was going to Mecca by way of Jeddah, whereas he really meant to go there by way of Yambu. If word of his plans should fall into a robber's ears—and it was very possible, almost certain—then he would wait in vain on the wrong road.

Burton had wondered how much four years of comparatively soft living in Europe had affected his endurance. There could hardly be a better test than riding eighty-four miles in the hot midsummer desert sun, on a bad wooden saddle on a vicious camel. He was right; his bones were to ache, and his skin would be burned black and raw by the sun beating through his thick robes. But the moment he was in the desert, he felt his spirits rise. The heat like a lion's breath, the pitiless and naked sky, the vast desolation and everpresent sense of insecurity and of death, these stimulated and sharpened Burton, so that, like a true Bedawin, he felt at home. Here, the keen air and the exercise were wine enough. In the desert, liquor only disgusted you. A man dropped the hypocrisies of civilization, became open-spoken, hospitable, and resolute. He loved the desert, and there were times when he thought of living the life of a Bedawin, among whom he would have been a chief.

A little later, he ran into Mohammed El Basyuni, the boy from whom he'd bought his pilgrim-clothes in Cairo. They traveled together, with Burton amused at the way this city Arab abused his desert kin. The next day they stopped under a mimosa tree to rest, and here Burton had his first trouble with a bunch of Maghrabi pilgrims. These were hungry and thirsty, and Burton, who really had a tender heart under his fierceness, gave each a pint of his water and same bread. The Maghrabis asked for more, which Burton could not spare. Then they cried out that they would take money instead. Burton thought that a few pence wouldn't hurt, but when they began demanding them and hinting that their knives might come out to enforce their demands, he took his pistols out. The pilgrims subsided.

At Suez Burton loaned money to his companions: Omar the Circassian, Saad the Devil, a Turk, Salih Sakkar and a Shaykh Hamid. Here Burton almost came to grief, for his boy Mohammed, in pawing thru his luggage, came across the sextant which Burton intended to use in making meteorological notes. When Burton was out of his room, Mohammed announced that this instrument proved that Abdullah was an infidel from India. The others, however, objected. Omar replied that Abdullah must be a very learned and devout Muslim, because he had several times answered questions about minute points of the faith which Omar himself did not know. Shaykh Hamid, thinking of the money he intended to borrow from Burton after they reached Mecca, cursed Mohammed for a pauper, an owl,[8] an excommunicate, a stranger, and a savage. Everybody heaped ashes on his head, but when Burton returned and found out what had gone on, he decided, sorrowfully, that the sextant had better remain behind. He could not afford even the slightest suspicion.

---

[8] Arabs believe that owls are a bad omen and if it hoots, your misfortune is even greater.

The pilgrims boarded the *Golden Wire*. This was a two masted *sambuk*, of about fifty tons, undecked, except upon the poop, which was high enough to act as a sail in a very strong wind. The captain had no means of reefing, nor a compass, log, sounding line, or chart. It was by guess and by Allah that he navigated.

On climbing aboard, Burton's heart sank. Ali Murad, the owner, had promised to allow only sixty passengers in the hold. And here were packed ninety-seven. Boxes and luggage were piled from stem to stern, and a group had established themselves on the poop, which was reserved for Burton and his friends. Saad the Devil, the giant slave, began clearing the deck in his simple forthright manner. He would pick up men by the scruff of their necks and toss them down into the hole below, along with their luggage, not caring whether a man landed on a box or a box on a man. There were still eighteen people on the poop, which was ten feet by eight. And the cabin was stuffed with fifteen men, women, and children. Down in the hold the same Maghrabis who had given Burton trouble were already scrapping with some Turks for elbow room. One of Burton's party, a Syrian, jumped down to restore order. At once he sank from view into the living sea. when fished out, his forehead was cut open, someone had snatched away half his beard, and sharp toothmarks were in the calf of his leg.

Daggers were drawn, and in a few minutes five men were seriously wounded. The fighting stopped. A delegation was sent ashore for Ali Murad to tell him the vessel was overcrowded. After three hours, he deigned to appear in a rowboat, and, staying well out of reach of any missile, said that anybody who wanted could leave and get his fare back. No one would go, so, after telling his passengers to trust in Allah and all would go well, Ali rowed off. At once, another brawl started. The Maghrabis demanded that the poop "aristocracy" relieve the pressure by taking a half a dozen from the hold.

Saad the Devil rose, cursed, and threw to his friends a bundle of *nebut*, thick ash staves, six feet long, well greased.

"Defend yourselves, if you don't wish to be the meat of the Maghrabis!" And to the savages, "Dogs and sons of dogs, now you shall see what the children of the Arab are!" His friends joined in. "I am Omar of Daghistan!" "I am Abdullah, the son of Joseph!"

The Maghrabi were not daunted by this naming of names; they swarmed like hornets towards the poop, shouting, "Allah Akbar!"

But the poop aristocracy had the advantage of being about four feet above them and their staves were longer than the enemies' palm sticks and short daggers. They began banging the savages on the heads; many reeled back with broken skulls.

Nevertheless, it took many hard blows to put a dent in those hard heads, and those who fell were trampled by their brothers, eager to get at the poop. Burton saw that they would shortly be overcome; looking around for something to help them his eyes lit on a large earthen jar full of drinking water, standing in its heavy wooden frame on the very edge of the poop. The whole contrivance must have weighed about a hundred pounds. Edging his way towards it so he wouldn't give away his plan, he suddenly shouldered it over the deck, and it rolled over on the heads below. Shrieks of pain and panic arose, for many were knocked down, and others were cut by the broken potshards or flooded in the water which burst forth. The Maghrabis withdrew to the other end of the ship.

Soon a delegation arrived from them suing for peace. Burton and his men agreed, on the condition that the Maghrabis take solemn vows not to make a disturbance again.

At Yambu they were told that the Hazimi tribe was harassing travelers. Burton decided to go on, anyway. He hired a litter, because it was easier to take notes in it than on a saddle on camelback. Besides, he had a sore foot as excuse for this woman's way of travel. This foot gave him much trouble the rest of the pilgrimage.

Every pilgrim carried a *hamail* or pocket Koran. It was hung in a red morocco case from silk cords hanging from the left shoulder. To conceal the fact he was taking notes and making sketches, Burton substituted an article that looked on the outside like a hamail. Inside were three compartments. One, for his watch and compass. The second, for money. The third, for penknife, pencils, and slips of paper, which he could hold concealed in the hollow of his hand. These were for drawing. He could always be writing his diary in the presence of the others by pretending to the illiterate that he was casting a horoscope for them or writing out a charm or that he was taking notes for a book of genealogy. To the curious Bedawin he would say, "And you, sons of Harb, on what ancestor do you pride yourselves?" And while they went into excruciating detail about their grandfather's ninth cousin, he would be writing on some other subject.

The caravan picked up other pilgrims. It had two hundred camels carrying grain, and an escort of seven irregular Turkish cavalry. Thieves attacked and were repelled with a few shots.

Later, they picked up an escort of two hundred men from a fort, but these returned when a band of Bedawin refused to allow the pilgrims to pass unless the soldiers left them. Later, another troop of Albanian soldiers joined the caravan, and they had a running fight with a band that fired on them from high rocks. Twelve soldiers were killed and many camels.

At Medinah, Burton visited Mohammed's supposed tomb and noted the legend that there is an empty place therein, reserved for Jesus after his second coming. According to the Muslim belief, Jesus will come again to announce the resurrection of Mohammed.

At a monument on Mount Ohod, which commemorated the place where the Prophet lost some front teeth by stoning from infidels, Burton, like any gawking tourist, wrote on the wall, "Abdullah, the servant of Allah," and beneath it the date according to Arabic numbering.

When the time came to go on, his friends urged him to stay and open a shop. He replied that he must make the pilgrimage required of every Muslim at least once in his life. "Goodbye, O Father of Moustachios," they said. "Peace be with you." Burton smiled at the nickname, for in Arabia everybody must be a father of something, and it was better to be the father of long whiskers than of a cooking-pot or a bad smell.

Shaykh Hamid came to him one morning after a visit at the

bazaar, and said, "You must make ready at once, Effendi. All Hajis start tomorrow. Allah will make it easy for you. Are your waterskins in order? You are to travel dawn the Darb El Sharki, where you will not see water for three days!"

Hamid was horror stricken, but Burton was happy. No European had ever traveled over the eastern road; besides, this was the path that the caliph famous in the Arabian Nights, Harun Al Rashid, had taken in company with the Lady Zubaydah, his wife.

Amid wild confusion, the caravan of seven thousand followers of the prophet plunged into the hellish desert. The rich rode on expensive saddles; the poor trudged barefooted. The camels, ponies, and asses began to drop under the terrific heat. Every mile seemed to add another carcass. The half-baked Takruri pilgrims, the poorest of the lot, would quickly cut the beast's throat to bleed it so that it would be religiously correct to eat it and then would cut out huge steaks which they would carry with them. Sometimes, the ever hovering vultures beat them to the carcass and so defiled it.

The sun became hotter and hotter. The scorching wind of the simoom struck; thin whirling columns of sand danced among them. Men would suddenly quiver and fall in their tracks and die and would be buried in a hastily scooped out shallow grave. Burton noticed that the Bedawin, though used to the desert, did not endure thirst any better than the others. Yet, though they often called out, "*Ya Latif*! (O merciful Lord!)" they bore their tortures like men and drank spoonfuls of clarified butter. Burton had the water-camel placed out in front so no one could steal water. Meanwhile, he observed that the more you drank under this sun, the more you wanted; your thirst just could not be satisfied. But if you could control the desire for the first two hours, you had won the battle, and to refrain from then on was easy.

Tempers grew exceedingly short. A Turk who could not speak a word of Arabic argued violently with an Arab who knew no Turkish. The Turk wished to add a few dry sticks to the camel's load; the Arab threw them off. Suddenly, the Turk struck the Arab. That night his stomach was ripped open with a dagger. Still living, he was wrapped in his shroud and placed in a half-dug grave. Burton did not see this interment, but he commented that it was a horrible way to die, for the sun would beat on the poor man's head all day, and at night the vultures and jackals would begin eating without bothering if he were still alive or not.

At El Zaribah the pilgrims bathed and put on ceremonial white robes with narrow red stripes, shaved their heads, trimmed their moustaches, and cut their nails. This latter was done so that they would not accidentally kill vermin while scratching themselves. And they were to leave their bald heads free of any covering from the hot sun, though they might form shade with their upraised hands.

Leaving El Zaribah, the caravan fell in with another from Baghdad. This was accompanied by about four hundred Wahahbis, all screaming, "Here I am!" and guided by a large loud kettledrum, marching in double file behind the standard bearer, whose green flag bore in white letters their creed. These mountaineers were wild and fierce looking, with hair twisted into thin plaits and carrying spears, matchlocks, and daggers. Their women despised veils and looked as tough as the men. When either sex saw a man smoking, they cursed him out as an infidel. Their camels were as wild as they and would dash through the caravan, creating confusion everywhere.

They plunged into a deep and stony valley. Everybody fell silent, as if expecting something gloomy. Suddenly, a small curl of smoke rose from a precipice to the right, and the dromedary just in front of Burton's fell dead, throwing his rider. There was a frightening confusion; men and animals jammed the narrow passage, all trying to get through. Bullets fell like rain into the solid mass. The irregulars tried to force their way through to attack. And the pasha in command, seeing that nothing could be done for the moment, spread his carpet at the foot of a cliff and argued with his officers about their strategy.

Then it was that Burton thought better of the Wahhabis, for, while one group fired on the Utaybah robbers, another charged up the hills. Presently the robbers fled, but panic overtook the caravan, and the wounded and dead were left behind, with many dead camels and much abandoned baggage.

At the beginning of the skirmish, Burton had primed his pistols and then calmly waited to see what he could do. Finding that there was nothing, he called out loudly for his supper.

The people around him exclaimed, "By Allah, he eats." Shaykh Abdullah, a man of better stuff, asked, "Are these Afghan manners?" Burton replied, "Yes, in my country we always dine before an attack of robbers, because those gentlemen are in the habit of sending men to bed supperless." The shaykh laughed, but the others looked offended. Burton thought that perhaps his bravado, typical of him, was too much for these people. But his words had made him a reputation and helped calm those around him.

After leaving the pass, the survivors hurried on. A day and a night passed with the tension mounting as they neared their goal. Then, at one A.M., Burton was awakened by cries of, "Mecca! Mecca!" Screaming for joy, weeping, the pilgrims passed through the *Bab El Salam*, the Gate of Security. From Medinah to Mecca, the journey of two hundred forty-eight English miles had been accomplished in eleven marches.

Burton stopped off briefly at the home of Mohammed. Then he hurried towards the last step of his pilgrimage: the House of Allah, a towering cubical building, in one corner of which was the holy black stone of the Ka'abah. He said the prayer for the unity of Allah, then made the seven circuits around the stone. Afterwards, the tremendous mob all rushed towards the stone to kiss it. Burton was in despair, because he could not get through them to study it. Finally, his boy Mohammed came to his rescue. Mohammed had been demonstrating his zeal by cursing every Persian in his path because they belonged to the heretical Shia sect. Besides, in 1674 A.D. some wretch had smeared the sacred stone with fecal matter so that those who rushed in to kiss it left with dirtied beards, and the Persians, unjustly, were accused or being defilers of the Ka'abah.

He now formed a flying wedge of six Meccans, and they bowled everybody out of their way. The Bedawin reached for their daggers, which they weren't allowed to carry in the holy city, and were knocked down. Burton took advantage of his husky guards to study the stone for at least ten minutes. If at this time he had been exposed for what he was, or even had there existed a bare suspicion, he would have been torn into bits by the crowd, pitched to the highest extreme of religious frenzy. Mohammed could have gained eternal glory by shouting out his suspicions that his master was the wicked white man who had disguised himself in India, "Ruffian Dick."

But the boy was either satisfied with Burton's disguise or else was thinking of the money he hoped to get from his master's stay. He never said a word and, for a while, at least, cooperated.

Burton, though studying the Ka'abah scientifically, at the same time shared in the same feelings as the most devout Muslim. To him it was as if the legend were true that the waving wings of angels were blowing the black curtains hung over the shrine. He thrilled with ecstasy. But, as he later confessed, part of the ecstasy was gratified pride at being the first infidel to have closely studied the holy black stone. Always the explorer, the man who wants to be first, he could not help being proud.

While kissing and rubbing his forehead on it, he narrowly examined the stone and concluded that it was a meteorite. It had fallen from the skies, been shattered, put together, and become a holy object long before Mohammed was born. The legend was that it had once been white but had become black because the sins of those who kissed it passed into it. Burton passed on to the holy well of Zem Zem and was drenched in foul-smelling water. Later that night he sneaked back to tear off a piece of the Ka'abah's curtain, but too many eyes were on him. However, with a coolness that some might have considered foolhardy, he took out a tape and measured the size of everything in which he was interested.

Burton went religiously through other ceremonies: the stoning of the Devil and the hearing of a sermon on Mount Arafat, where Eve was first supposed to have set foot on earth. During the latter, he began a flirtation with a very nicely shaped girl whose eyes looked beautiful through her mask of muslin. She made signs favorable to him; her chaperone seemed unaware. All was going fine; then she became lost in the crowd.

The next day, word came to him to appear at the Ka'abah. Bareheaded, barefooted, he appeared in the square. A crowd was there, but at the cry, "Open a path for the Haji who would enter the House," they made way. Two sturdy Meccans lifted him up to a third, who drew him into the building. He was questioned very sternly about his name, nation, and other particulars. Though apprehensive, Burton answered correctly, and the boy Mohammed was told to conduct him around the building and say the prayers. Burton, looking at the windowless walls, the officials at the door, and the crowd below, felt like a trapped rat. Any unorthodox action, a misjudged prayer or bow, and he'd have been crucified or perhaps impaled in a peculiarly painful manner. Nevertheless, he made careful observations and penciled a rough sketch on his white robe. Then he passed from the big black house shaped like a cubical coffin, having done that which many who made the pilgrimage had not. For the majority could not afford it, since those who walked the holy floor could never again tell lies, and lying was the breath of life to the Oriental.

There were other visits and ceremonies which he made; but he was impatient to get out of Mecca. His purse was almost empty, and his room was hot as an oven. He took a caravan to Jeddah, where he appeared at the British Consulate. He was left to cool his heels for a long time. He heard someone say, "Let the dirty n—— wait." When he finally did get in, he gave the consul a piece of paper, supposed to be a money order. He had written on it, "Don't recognize me. I am Dick Burton, but I am safe yet. Give me some money, which will be returned from London. Don't take any notice of me."

Burton went back to Egypt. World wide fame waited for him because of his exploit. His book, *A Pilgrimage to El-Medinah and Meccah*, was to become one of the greatest books of travel. Not only the West praised him, but the East too, because he had performed the pilgrimage with devoutness, and was a true Haji. He could have seized the chance to make money and become a social and literary lion. Any other man would have done it, but Burton had a fatal sense of mistiming. Time and again he was to be on the brink of his dreams; only to refuse to appear to gather his rewards or else to go off on another expedition. At this time he could have made a huge success in England with lectures and interviews. All kinds of wild stories about him were circulating; it was said he had stabbed a Muslim who had penetrated his disguise.

But he had a peculiar and fierce pride. His discoveries could speak for themselves. He would stay in Egypt to write his book. He would also brood over his *Kasidah* a long philosophical poem setting forth his dark and pessimistic views on life and death and chance and God. It sounds much like the *Rubaiyat* of Omar Khayyam and was written, though not published, years before Fitzgerald's famous translation.

His leave was up. He went back to his regiment at Bombay. Again, he became restless and unhappy. There was the city of Harar in the eastern horn of Africa, behind whose walls no infidel had ever been. What lay behind them?

The Royal Geographical Society, also interested, backed the now famous captain. The East India Company, more than ever suspicious of Ruffian Dick, gave him permission, provided he went as a private traveler and asked them for no funds. Perhaps the directors hoped he would end up on a spear this time and finish their trouble-maker for good.

Burton didn't care. All he wanted was cooperation; he would provide the brains and the guts. And, of course, he wasn't even to get a minimum of help. Only misunderstanding and deliberate fouling-up from his inferiors.

"The city of Harar will fall when a Frank (European) enters it," ran one proverb. And another: "As soon enter a crocodile's mouth as the walls of Harar."

Despite this, thirty Europeans had from time to time tried to go into Harar; all had died. Richard Burton would be the thirty-first to try; death and proverbs were a challenge to him.

The East India Company had long wanted to explore eastern

Ethiopia. Berberah, the chief port of Somaliland, was the safest and best harbor on the western side of the Indian Ocean, much better than Aden, across the Gulf. When Richard offered to fill out the big blank area on their maps, they eagerly agreed. But cautiously. He could go as a private traveler and would get no protection from the government. Agreed. He selected three men, Lts. Herne and Speke of the army, Lt. Stroyan of the Indian Navy. But as usual, he ran into obstacles from the first. Not from the natives but from his fellow Englishmen. Sir James Outram, the political resident at Aden, opposed the expedition because he thought it would stir up the Somalis, and he told George Buist, the editor of the *Bombay Times*, to run down the project.

Burton had to change his plans because of the continued vehemence of the resident against his plans. The original route was to have been from Berberah westwards to Harar, and then southeast to Zanzibar. Instead Speke was told to land in the harbor of Goree Bunder, where he would trace the watershed of the Wadi Nogal, buy horses and camels, and collect red earth that might contain gold. Unfortunately, his guide proved treacherous, so Speke's plans failed. Herne was to go to Berberah, where he would meet Stroyan.

Burton chose the most dangerous mission—although the most glorious if it succeeded. Disguised as an Arab merchant, he would go to Harar. Bad news came at once. On landing at Zayla, he was told that the friendship between the Amir of Harar and the governor of Zayla had broken up. The road through the Easa tribe had been closed up because of the murder of Masud, the governor's adopted son. All strangers had been thrown out of Harar because one of them had misbehaved. And smallpox was raging so furiously in the city that the Galla peasants around it would allow no one in or out.

Nevertheless, Burton went ahead. Though the governor, Sharmarkay, knew who Burton was, he pretended to accept him as an Arab. For twenty-six days he stayed at Sharmarkay's home, while be lived religiously as a devout Muslim and also chose his caravan retinue. These might have stepped out of the *One Thousand and*

One Nights. They were El Hammal, or The Porter, a bullnecked, lamp-black sergeant of the Aden police. Guled, called Long, a tall living skeleton of a policeman. Abdy Abokr, the End of Time. Abdy was a catlike, long-backed hedge-priest with a villainous grin and close-set eyes. His title came from the prophecy that the end of the world would find every Muslim priest totally corrupt, and he seemed to fit that description.

With his servants and some mules and camels, he set out on November 27th, 1854. Every person there was a character, even the camels had individuality; one was so mean and noisy that he at once was called El Harami, the Ruffian. Raghe, their Easa guide, strode first, bearing in one hand a spear and in the other a round leather shield. Behind him waddled the two female cooks, each large as three average women rolled into one, muscular and enormously hipped. They were stronger than the men, and did the work of four. Once they got over their first shyness with Burton, they began making jokes with him that would have made a camel-driver blush. When they became tired at the end of the day, one would lie down and the other would walk barefooted on her back, kneading with her toes. Then she would rise, refreshed.

Their attendant, Yusuf, was one-eyed, and nicknamed the Kalendar, after the cyclopean porter in the Arabian Nights. He was highly moral and wished to discipline the two cooks with sticks. Only Burton's harsh orders kept him from beating them to death; they hated Yusuf's guts, and waited for a chance to revenge themselves.

Behind them, the camels, then the three policemen on horses, with their greased frizzled wigs, new spears and shields. No guns for them, for here in Somaliland they would be laughed at for such outlandish weapons.

Behind them, Burton, on a fine white mule, a double-barreled gun across his lap, and two pairs of holsters, holding his Colt six-shooters.

They traveled due south along the coast through a hard stone-less plain, now muddy, now dry, and through flats of black mold powdered with salt. The second day, they came to a village where the Bedawin gathered around and muttered, "Faranj! (Frank!)" and laughed at their weapons. Burton waited his chance; then, when a large vulture settled on the ground, he shot it. Loading his gun with swan-shot, he shot another as it flew over. Screams of admiration rose; a graybeard, putting his finger in his mouth, called, "Praise Allah! May he defend me from such a calamity!"

Pleased with the effect he'd made, Burton decided that from then on one barrel would always be loaded with shot. Next day, the old man asked for a charm to cure his sick camel. Burton gave it to him and had to listen to a speech of thanks that took half an hour. Afterwards, the old man spat on everybody in the caravan to give them good luck. Burton endured this, for it was well in this country to get along with the old men, who were looked up to by their tribesmen.

A few days later they fell in with a tribe that was migrating. One of the Somali fell in love with the huge cook Scheherezade, and asked her to marry him. She delayed saying no, but didn't dare come out with a flat refusal for fear of angering him and his fellows, one hundred and fifty spearsmen. The suitor then suggested that the marriage ceremony was really unimportant. The others grew sulky because Burton had not passed out enough tobacco to suit them. Just before leaving, he sent the mules out to water, and when they did not come back, he thought the Bedawin had seized them. He sat on a cow's hide in the sun and ordered his men to load their guns. Loudly, he threatened the culprits with death by witchcraft if they were bothered. The old man then declared that it was not good to detain these strangers; the mules came back, but the escort Burton had asked for was not forthcoming. He pushed on without them.

The footprints of a large Habr Awal cavalcade lay in the dust before them. The servants huddled together, silent; the End of Time spoke hollowly, "Verily, O pilgrim, who so seeth the track, seeth the foe!" Though despising their cowardice, Burton felt uneasy, for they were nine against two hundred horsemen. Fortunately, they soon came to very rough country, where the natives would not care to endanger their horses.

The plain faded behind them; the mountains lay before them, and the jujube began growing tall. They met some wild Gudabirsi, and from them Burton learned how fast the grapevine worked even in these far-off hills. They talked of the latest battles of the Russian war, and he heard of a storm which had wrecked ships in the Bombay harbor, only a few weeks after it happened.

Later, some Gudabirsi tried to seize Raghe, declaring he owed them a cow. Burton fired a pistol over their heads, and they cringed like dogs. Poor Raghe was in a bad spot because he was in a country with whose people his had a blood-feud. He feared to sleep in their villages, yet he could not sleep outside because of the lions.

They met some Abbans, and having heard from them that they knew of a place where elephants were thick as sand, he went hunting. The End of Time rode with them, but he lagged behind. And he looked so miserable on hearing that a mule cannot outrun an elephant that Burton sent him back to their kraal.

"Do you believe me to be a coward, O Pilgrim?" said the hedge-priest.

"Of a truth I do," replied Burton.

The End of Time rode away, saying, "What has a man but a single life? And he who throws it away, what is he but a fool?"

Burton found no elephants and returned to camp disappointed.

They rode on. The Bedawin they met repeatedly said, "They will spoil that white skin of yours at Harar."

On the 23rd of December they descended to the Marar prairie. This the Eesa, Berteri, and Habr Awal made a happy hunting grounds for robbers. A traveler burst in on the caravan. Naked, he had escaped from the savages with nothing but his life. Late at dusk, Burton riding as rear guard, noticed his mule prick up its ears. Looking back, he saw a large animal, following stealthily. His companions would not fire, because they thought it might be a man, but he shot—missing because of the new moon's weak light—and scared off a huge lion. He got another chance to notice the cowardice of his friends, for they ran about, tossing their hands in the air, and talked of nothing but the lion the rest of the night.

At Wilensi, Burton was busy settling arguments between El Hammal and the End of Time. The latter was getting bigheaded because he'd been made ambassador to the Girhi chief by the governor of Zaylah. He wanted to command the whole caravan. The two buxom cooks begged to be left behind. They were afraid that the smallpox raging at Harar might make them ugly. Burton, though thinking that they could not become any uglier than they were, ordered the one-eyed Kalendar to remain behind to guard them. He marched on to the village of Gerad Adan, a chief. Here he came down with the colic and thought that he would die. For five days he lay, while the Gerad went off to Harar for millet beer as medicine. This powerful drink would surely have killed him, for it was mixed with a poisonous bark, and affected even the hardened natives with splitting headaches. The Gerad's daughters sacrificed a sheep for his recovery; the Galla Christians crowded around him and wept for him because he was going to die far from his fatherland, under a tree.

Nothing would have been easier, but Burton could not endure the thought of such an ignoble death. To go down under a charge of savage spearsmen was one thing; to perish of colic, ridiculous.

He rose, dressed in his Arab best, and prepared to push on. Five strangers appeared; they took the Gerad aside and advised him that Burton was a spy and should be sent as prisoner to the Amir of Harar. The Gerad replied that he did not betray his friends.

Nevertheless, the Gerad was afraid of his Harari kinsmen and refused to escort Burton. The End of Time, almost fainting with fright, begged to remain behind; Burton granted permission.

He then made a speech to his two faithful soldiers: Boldness was the word from now on. He would take off his Arab disguise and openly proclaim his true identity. They would ride into Harar behind no false faces. He would present a letter which he had written himself, but which purported to be from the English resident at Aden. He mounted and rode forward, while the villagers recited the prayer of the Fatihah for the dead.

When they mounted the crest of a hill and saw Harar, his

companions looked at each other in wonder. Were they facing death for this somber pile of stones? But Burton was exultant, for none of those who had gone before him had succeeded in entering. And he was sure that he would at least get in.

They did, and there the warder of the gate told them to dismount and to follow him at a trot. Burton refused, because he would look undignified. After a delay, during which he declined to part with his dagger and revolver, he marched through a double line of tall scowling Gallas, each holding a spear with a blade broad as a shovel. He went through a curtain and stood before the feared chief.

The Amir sat in a dark room on whose whitewashed walls hung rusty matchlocks and polished fetters. He was a young, small man with a yellow complexion, frowning forehead, and bulging eyes.

Burton entered, loudly saying, "Peace be upon you!"

The Amir answered graciously enough and held out a bony hand, like a kite's claw. Two men grabbed Burton's arms and bowed him over the hand. But he would not kiss it, and, after a minute, he was released. His two servants then kissed the chief's hand twice.

"What is your errand?" asked the Amir. He glanced briefly at the letter and demanded further explanation. Burton said that he had come to Harar with the compliments of the governor of Aden and also to see the light of the Amir's countenance.

There was a pause. Burton scarcely breathed, though he kept his face composed. The many relatives and courtiers watched the chief's face to see how they should react. The matchlock men held their burning fuses in their hands; let the Amir command, and they would tear the Frank apart with their huge musketballs. And if, inconceivable thought, they should miss, the Galla spearsmen gathered behind Burton would plunge their blades into his back. But Burton resolved that if he had to, he would run up to the throne and hold his pistol against the Amir's head.

Suddenly, the Amir smiled. Burton relaxed a little, and soon he was in the second palace, which would be his home as long as he lived in Harar. Where there had been frowns, there were now smiles, but he knew that they could as swiftly change back. Burton sent a revolver as a present to the chief, and began making himself comfortable.

He was to spend ten days in Harar, largely monotonous, except for the overtones of fear and insecurity. At any time the Amir could have changed his mind, and as he was notoriously fickle even among a fickle people, there was never any assurance that the next day would find Burton alive.

He examined the city, found it to be one mile long by a half a mile wide. The wall had many holes in it, through which wild beasts sometimes crept at night. He could not make even a single note, because he was so closely watched. Afterwards, he compiled from memory a grammar of the Harari language. It was, he noted, spoken only within the walls and was not Arabic but was related to Amharic. The citizens hated all foreigners with a holy zeal, Muslims as well as Christians. Both men and women were very loose in their morals, and everybody was drunk as often as they could get their hands on alcohol of any kind.

Some Habr Awals came to the Vizier and told him that spies were waiting at Berberah for the return of their brother from Harar. These were, of course, Speke, Herne, and Stroyan. Summoned to the Vizier's house to answer these charges, Burton found the old man sick with bronchitis. He at once made him feel better by burning under his nose brown paper matches steeped in saltpeter. He also promised to send him enough medicine from Aden to last his life. Won by this, the Vizier promised to intercede with the Amir for Burton, even though he might lose his own head. He had his chance in a short time, for the Amir sent for him. Not long after, Burton was also called. They had a long conversation about what the English were doing in Arabia. Reassured as to their own intentions towards him, the Amir smiled his rare smile and gave Burton permission to leave. Perhaps he thought that Burton might send down a doctor to him, too, for he suffered from tuberculosis.

The Englishman had been hearing too much recently about the dungeon beneath the palace, where a man went down alive but never came up so. He said a short prayer for the Amir, and retired. At the palace, he whispered to his two comrades, "Achcha! (All right!)"

A few days later, he rode away. But on the road back to Berberah, they lost their way, following their incompetent guide. The sun beat on them; they dared not drink from their almost empty water bags. Burton became delirious with visions of water bubbling icily over the rocks. Half-conscious, he realized that he had ridden twenty-four hours without water. Even twelve hours in the desert without water was generally enough to kill a man. A few more hours, and they would drop in their tracks, food for the vultures and hyenas. Thirty-six hours passed without water. The twilight of the tropics rushed towards them. Then he saw a *katta*, a sand-grouse, flying towards the hills. These birds had to drink at least once a day; this one must be making for water. The party, hearing Burton's cry, took heart and followed the bird. A hundred yards away was a spring, which they would surely have missed. All plunged their heads into the water, too mad with thirst to pay any attention to the swarm or insects and tadpoles, and drank till they were likely to burst. Burton never again shot a katta.

When they reached Berberah, the natives swore aloud that they could not have ridden from Harar in five days. Such a thing was impossible.

Though the weather was bad, Burton got upon a native boat and ordered in loud voice that the sail be set for Aden.

The crew and passengers raised a hubbub. "He surely will not sail in a sea like this?" asked the captain.

"He will," replied El Hammal.

"It blows wind," protested the captain.

"And if it blew fire?" said the Arab, meaning that the Frank was crazy enough to sail into anything.

The captain and a soldier invaded Burton's cabin, still protesting. He grabbed the former by his beard and pants' seat and threw him out on the deck.

At Aden he picked up men for another expedition to Harar and returned to Berberah, where he was attacked by the Somali and speared through the jaw. On sick leave again, he returned to England in 1855. Now was his chance to get into the limelight, the chance he had thrown away when he had stayed in Egypt after the Mecca pilgrimage. The Harar expedition was an even greater feat, and the fight outside Berberah, attested to by the two scars on his face, would have been a crashing climax to his lecture.

But fate, the ironical bitch who seemed to have it in for Burton, chose that time to drown out everything else of interest with the Crimean War. Nobody had ear for anything personal; it must be on the grand scale and on the Russian-British front. He finished his book, *First Footsteps in East Africa*, and then volunteered. Not being able to get the commission he wanted from the War Office, he took ship to Constantinople. There he got an appointment as chief of staff of the Bashi-Bazouks, Turkish irregular cavalry. The four thousand wild Albanians knew nothing of discipline, of morning roll calls or drilling. Their favorite amusement was dueling, in which the contestant would stand with a glass of araki in one hand and a pistol in the other. He who first emptied his glass banged away at the other. Not only that, but the British officers knew nothing of the use of the sword they carried. He could do little about the duels except insure fair play, but he did teach the English saber play and he soon had organized the troopers into a fairly well-disciplined and dependable outfit.

At that time the city of Kars, held by the Turks, was being besieged by the Russians. Despite famine and light numbers, they were holding out bravely. Burton conceived the plan of galloping to the city's relief with his Bashi-Bazouks. Inspired, he rode to Constantinople, where he laid his brilliant idea before the English Ambassador.

Lord Stratford grew purple-faced. "By God, sir, you are the most impudent man in the Bombay army!" he roared.

That was the only answer he got. Bewildered, Burton left. Months later, he discovered that the high statesmen of England and France had decided that Kars should be allowed to fall, a sort of peace offering to Russia, salve for her loss of Sebastopol. And he, only a captain, had almost upset some very delicate undercover work of the great men.

Nevertheless, Stratford must have been impressed, for he commissioned Burton to visit Schamyl. Schamyl was the Circassian who was leading his mountain country in a revolt against Russia. This was just the sort of mission to appeal to Burton, for he would have to disguise himself and ride through Russian territory to get to Circassia. But there was one problem, what would he say to Schamyl?

"Oh, say you are sent to report to me," replied Stratford.

"But, my lord, Schamyl will expect money, arms, and possibly troops. What am I to reply if he asks me about it? Otherwise, he might take me for a spy, and my chance of returning to Constantinople will be uncommonly small."

Lord Stratford could promise nothing, so Burton regretfully refused the useless mission. Schamyl and his country would later be crushed, a victim of high-powered diplomacy, as Kars had been. Given English support, Circassia might have held off Russia for a long time, perhaps remained independent. Years later, a young man was to come out of this area and become ruler of Russia. If Circassia had been free, he might have stayed there. In his native mountains he was called Djugashvil. Russians knew him as Stalin.

As usual, Burton's talents were wasted; he would never fight on a battlefront. All his actions would be personal, confined to his superiors.

Burton resigned and went back to London, where he dreamed again of tearing aside the veil of Isis, of discovering the true source of the Nile. Many men had tried and failed, but, he noted, they had started at the end of the river and worked up to its beginning. Characteristically, he would ignore the common route and would slash through from the side. Inland from the coast of East Africa would be his path. Did not the Arabs talk of a Sea of Ujiji? Might not this fabled great lake give birth to the Nile in the hot heart of the Dark Continent?

The Royal Geographical Society talked the Foreign office and the East India Company into granting him a thousand pounds and two years' leave of absence. With Speke, now a captain, he landed on the island of Zanzibar at the end of 1856. There was little reason why he should have chosen Speke, for the man knew no Arabic nor Swahili, and he was not a scientist. He was brave, but from all indications he would be more of a hindrance than a help, in a country where Burton would need all the aid he could get. It was almost as if Burton had taken steps to defeat himself.

But beneath his roaring voice, iron face, and fierce black eyes, Burton was kind and fair minded. He knew that Speke had suffered in East Africa, and that he wanted a chance to explore again. What he did not know was that Speke secretly resented him, nursing the inevitable hatred of the mediocrity.

They were to take along his old friend, Doctor Steinhauser. This man loved Burton and his medical knowledge would help them through the fevers they knew they'd catch. Unfortunately, it was the doctor who fell too sick to go along, not Speke. Unable to wait past the middle of May for him to recover, the two set out.

From the beginning, he had trouble. His Balochi mercenaries and native porters were rogues, thieves, and cowards to the last man. The porters would carry only the lightest of loads, leaving the heavy on the ground. Burton used threats, pleas, and a whip; it was the latter that decided them; they could carry their loads after all. But many were scared by the tales of the dangers they would run across: poisoned arrows of the bush Negroes, the deadly long horned rhinoceros, mad elephants. One hundred and seventy carriers had been hired, but only thirty-six were brave enough to show up for work. The others fled into the jungle with their advance pay. Burton had to hire others.

Lack of money troubled him from the very start. If he had had five thousand pounds, he could have hired a hundred matchlock men and had enough to pay the tribute that every chief they met would expect. They could even have marched through the country of the Masai, now on the warpath. But the kind of safari he wanted would have cost at least a hundred pounds a week; six weeks, and his money would be gone.

To add to his handicaps, he received a letter from the East India Company, ordering him to return to London, where he would be a witness in a court martial. Though he knew that a court martial might be his own fate if he disobeyed, he decided to ignore the command. No matter what the consequences, he could not abandon the expedition now, would not be thwarted a second time. On June 26th, 1857, he gave the signal. Their guide raised his blood red flag, which always marched in the front of a Zanzibar caravan, kettledrums and cowbells boomed and clanged, porters yelled with excitement, and the procession lurched into the jungle like a drunken and monstrous land-serpent.

In eighteen days they marched one hundred and eighteen miles. Their Zanzibar asses, too delicate for this climate, died. They were forced to use the half-wild Wamyamwezi beasts. Many of these were killed by hyenas, so bold they would bite off the faces of the men as they slept at night. Always, every chief they met assumed he would be given gleaming beads and bolts of precious cloth. Everywhere lay clean-picked skeletons and the swollen corpses of porters who had starved to death. Smallpox, famine and slavers stalked the land; one place had so many graves that it was called the Valley of Death and the Home of Hunger. Sick natives died where they fell, abandoned by their families to the vulture and the fox. Witch hunts were terrorizing every village. Men and women were burnt at stakes, and their children, guilty by association, were also cast onto the flames.

At Dut'humi, one chief had kidnapped five subjects of another chief. Though sick, Burton organized a counter raiding party and brought the unhappy ones back home.

Malaria brought Richard down for twenty days. Delirious, he saw himself as two men, each fighting against the other, forever scheming against and tripping the other up. This strong sense of a divided personality attacked him during his fever fits throughout his life. It was not just wild dreams but a real clue to his true character. Burton *was* two; he was forever defeating himself when just on the verge of victory.

And he must have cursed during this time of weakness and feverish hallucinations. He was a cursing man; it is probable that the malaria released his inhibitions and that during this time, Speke heard much of what caused this splitting of personality and

Speke learned the true source of his psychological injury. Just as later, Speke would become sick and in his ravings reveal his secret hatred for Burton.

Burton must have cursed many times during his life because of what his mother had done to him. If she had not so hatefully and stubbornly resisted his grandfather's changing his will, he would have been a rich man. Wealthy, he could have organized expeditions that would not have been crippled from the start. The time would come when Stanley and Baker and Grant and Cameron[9] would be famous names on everybody's lips. Yet Burton was the greatest of all nineteenth century explorers and stands at the very top of the list of the greatest of all time. Where the other men of his day had plenty of money to hire supplies and soldiers and tribute goods, he had to forge practically alone. Given the fortune that should have been his, he could have mapped most of the huge white blank in Africa's dark heart years before anybody else. Even so, what he did was magnificent. For instance, his chartings of routes in East Africa and Arabia were used by World War I soldiers. Stanley took one book along in his travels. Not the Bible, as reported, but Burton's *Lake Regions of Central Africa.* And Lawrence of Arabia declared that Burton's description of the pilgrim's route from Medina to Mecca was correct to the least detail.

Moreover, as money talks, his fortune would have influenced the snobs of the Foreign Office to give him the consular posts that he deserved, instead of the third rate ones to be tendered him. There is little doubt that with the proper sort of backing his money would have brought him, he would have gotten the viceroyship of India or the general-governership of Egypt. If he'd

[9] **Sir Henry Morton Stanley** (1841-1904) was a Welsh journalist, explorer, soldier, author and politician who was famous for his exploration of central Africa, and his search for missionary and explorer David Livingstone.

Sir Samuel White Baker (1821-1893) was an English explorer, officer, and abolitionist. He is mostly remembered as an explorer of the Nile and interior of central Africa.

Lieutenant-Colonel James Augustus Grant (1827-1892) was a Scottish explorer of eastern equatorial Africa. Grant's gazelle, one of the largest and handsomest of that family in Africa, was named in his honor.

Verney Lovett Cameron (1844-1894) was an English traveller in Central Africa and the first European to cross (1875) equatorial Africa from sea to sea.

had the later post, England's relations with her province of the Nile might have been different. No Khartoum, no massacre of "Chinese" Gordon.

All this was *if* . . . He did not have the great fortune; his mother had preferred to cheat her son so that her adored half-brother might gamble it away and give it to confidence men.

It is strange that none of his biographers have noted such an obvious breeding ground for mental wounds or for the birth of some of his twisted attitudes. Nobody, not even his wife in her two-volume *Life* mentioned that possibility. It is probable he never spoke of it to anyone, but there must have been times when he felt how keenly his poverty had robbed him of the success he deserved; an angry man, he could not have repressed into total unconsciousness the tide of fury against his mother.

In his fever-deliriums, hags pursued him. Were these symbols of how he really felt about her? In waking life, he was always flirting with pretty women; his tremendous masculinity and overpowering personality assured him success with the fair sex wherever he went. But his contempt for them was well known. He thought they were, by and large, a brainless silly deceptive back-biting lot. Never once did he see that this view exactly described his male enemies, who were always opposing him. Whereas he never considered that most women, except for his mother, helped him.

All old women, he stated, looked like apes. And when the ladies asked him to autograph one of his books, he would write in Arabic: "I stood before the gates of Paradise, and lo! most of its inmates were the poor; and I stood before the gate of Hell, and lo! most of its inmates were women!"

There is a good chance that when he was expressing his sarcasms towards the generality of womankind, he had his mother in mind. Burton, though no gentleman in the conventional meaning of the term, preferred pretty blue-eyed blondes with bird brains. His mother's likeness? It matches her description. The fact that he had a passion for blondes, instead of hating them, does not disprove this theory. What a man's unconscious mind hates, his conscious often loves. And vice versa. A pioneer in hypnotism, he liked to put them under the spell of his gleaming black eyes and make them do ridiculous things. He forced his wife to be his favorite subject. She was herself one of the pretty yellow-haired types, though no dimwit. And she gave him what he had lacked in his real mother, an all-worshiping hovering slave-like love. Too much so, in fact, for Burton, the man of extremes, had picked out a woman who almost smothered him with devotion.

It was shortly after his grandfather had dropped dead on his way to change the will that Richard's red hair and blue eyes became gypsy-black. Chameleonlike, he was two persons, the man he showed to intimates, the soft-spoken, gay, tender, warm fellow, and the man he showed to the outside world, the loud, swaggering, bragging, monstrously lying, almost savage fellow. He was split right down the middle; he dreaded snakes but forced himself to play with cobras and like it; he had a horror of graveyards and corpses, yet he could collect cholera-ridden carcasses in a cart and help pile them in a dump; he could face one hundred and fifty howling spearsmen with only a saber, but he could not stand to say "goodby," the word was so taboo to him that even when he thought of saying it he broke out into a trembling and a cold sweat; he could get so dangerously drunk that he would stagger home with a revolver clutched in his hand, frightening all in his path, yet he nursed the famous explorer Cameron, and the poet Swinburne with such loving care that they declared him the gentlest and kindest of men and worshipped him as a superman. He believed absolutely in nothing spiritual, was deeply pessimistic, yet he spent half his life becoming more adept in various religions than any except the most fanatic.

His very face betrayed his character. As Swinburne was to say, he had the "brow of a god and the jaw of a devil."

All of this was shown by the delirium-images when he came down with twenty-two bouts of malaria during this expedition. But he survived the one at Dut'humi and rose to go on.

Speke suffered sunstroke. Yet they rode on, so weak they could hardly sit on their saddles. Then a stay at the Usagara

Mountains helped them recover their strength. They continued. Burton became sick again. He sent Speke on ahead to a village to get a hammock for him. Speke failed to send it back, so Burton remounted. The caravan had been held up by an attack of wild bees. They passed through villages destroyed by slavers and found two who had escaped the man-hunters lurking in the jungles. Horse-ants bit them so they danced like the chorus of a comic opera; then tsetse flies, which could bite through a hammock. At Rubeho, the third range of the Usagara, they met a caravan of Arabs. These, like all their countrymen, hailed Burton as one of their own and fed him milk and honey.

Up the mountains they went, Speke so weak three men had to hold him up. Burton, the stronger, only needed one. Suddenly, the war cry rang out, and long files of savage Wahumbas appeared. The two white men were too weak to rise, and their soldiers and porters crouched, ready to run off. But for some unknown reason, the Wahumba ignored them, probably intent on their bloodfeud with the Inengé, dwellers in the plains.

At Great Rubeho, Speke became so violent that Burton had to take his guns away from him. The tawny-haired Englishman appeared to have suffered permanent brain damage from this attack.

Reports came that some Arabs were preceding them with tales that the whites were wizards come to ruin the land. The chiefs became more hostile and bolder, demanding more tribute. Though an attack on their part would have crumpled the weak caravan, Burton packed his animals and ordered them to stand to one side. They cringed.

The hundred and thirty-fourth day after leaving the coast, they entered Kazeh. Here they stayed for a long time, while Burton felt at home among the Muslims stationed there. Speke, who knew none of the languages, became soured at this isolation and also aggressive, probably because he felt guilty about his own increasing incompetency. A fresh gang of porters were hired, but these were as lazy, cowardly, and dishonest as the others. Again, they set out. And Burton had to watch every man, for there was not a one who did not, sooner or later, try to desert.

Nevertheless, they admired Burton. He was Muzungu Mbaya, "the wicked white man." To have been called the "good white man" was to be considered a weak fool, one ripe for the plucking.

> "We will follow Muzungu Mbaya," they sang.
> "Puti! puti! (Grub! grub!)
> As long as he gives us good food!
> Puti! puti!
> We will traverse the hill and the stream,
> Puti! puti!
> With the caravan of this great *mundewa* (merchant).
> Puti! puti!"

A partial paralysis took hold of him, creeping upward from his feet. His ribs felt as if they were caving in, then the attack stopped. In ten days the numbness had passed from hands and feet, but it would be over a year before he could walk a long distance.

They passed quickly and quietly through a land laid waste by the fierce Watuta. On the 13th of February, Burton saw his *fundi* or leader change their direction. They went up a hill so steep Speke's ass, the only good one they had, dropped dead, and the other beasts were too tired to follow. "What is that streak of light below?" he said to Sidi Bombay.

"I think it is *the* water you are looking for," replied Bombay.

Burton's heart sank. Was this little lake the Ujiji that the Arabs said was so great a sea? He cursed them for liars and thought of returning at once to explore the Nyanza.

But he walked a few yards further, and on his half-blinded eyes burst a glorious vision, the immensity and beauty of Lake Tanganyika. Suddenly, he thrilled with the knowledge that all their hardships had been worth it, and that he was the first European to have reached the headwaters of the Nile. Isis lay unveiled before him in all her beauty.

The whole caravan joined in his ecstasy. Only Speke, blind, grumbled he could see nothing because of the mist and glare. On a dhow hired from an Arab merchant, they set out on the fabled sea. His triumph disappeared under new sicknesses brought on by the cold damp, and the fish and vegetables, which they ate too much of. Speke had an affliction which made him chew sideways, like a cow with her cud. Too ill even to talk, Burton sent Speke to the northern end of the lake, from which a large river was supposed to flow northwards. There he was to hire a dhow for a month's cruise. Twenty-seven days later, Speke returned, with rusty guns, wet powder, and nothing but a promise that after three months they could get the boat for five hundred dollars. This was the same dhow whose owner had previously promised Burton he could have it as soon as he wanted it. Though disgusted with him, Burton helped him write out his diaries. He was surprised to see that Speke had traced a vast horseshoe shaped range of mountains in a place which he knew had only a thin ridge of hills. Later Speke published the map in Blackwood's magazine and stated the little hills were the true Mountains of the Moon.

Burton bribed Kannena, a chief, and got two canoes and fifty-five men. With these he sailed for a month up and down the two hundred and fifty mile long Tanganyika. His tongue got an ulceration which made him unable to speak for a long time. But the end of the trip found him far healthier than the beginning. The rainy monsoon broke up; at the same time, though, Burton had to begin digging into his own pocket to pay his men. A caravan arrived with letters from Europe. Now he first learned of the Indian mutiny against which he had vainly warned the authorities years before.

He had planned on exploring the southern end of Lake Tanganyika, then returning to Zanzibar by Nyassa Lake and Kilwa. But the goods sent by his agent via the caravan were too poor for him to hire porters for that long trip. Nevertheless, he was happy to leave on the back trail, May 26, 1858.

When they halted at Kazeh again, Burton had fallen sick once more. Speke felt better, because the burden of the expedition had fallen on his leader. During their stay at Kazeh, they had heard from Arabs of a large lake lying sixteen marches to the north. Burton decided to send Speke to investigate. There was no need for both of them to go, and he did not want to leave him behind, for Speke could not talk to any of the natives. Moreover, there were other preparations only Burton could make before they started their journey homeward.

On the 25th of August Speke came back, bursting with the news that the lake was much larger than expected. And, much more important, that he had discovered the *true* source of the White Nile!

Again Fate, that yellow-haired and smiling bitchgoddess, had struck Burton when he was on the verge of success. She had handed the prize, won through such sufferings and effort, to a man who had ridden as a parasite on his back all the way from Zanzibar.

Burton would not, could not, believe it. He listened to Speke's story. The geography given by Speke did not ring true, and part of the man's belief was based on the testimony of Arabs not known for their reliability. It was too much to swallow. He made up his mind that Speke was wrong, and he never changed it to the end of his days.

But Speke was right.

On the way back, they spoke only when they must. Once again, disease struck. Speke was attacked by the *kichyomachyoma*, the "little irons," so called because it felt like many knives sticking into a man's sides. Wild beasts and lionheaded demons seemed to attack him; he foamed at the mouth and barked like a dog, cramps made him rigid as wood, spasm after spasm shook him. Burton did not leave his bedside for days, nursing him tenderly. All this despite the fact that the delirious man raved his secret hatred for Burton. Nor was he grateful to his leader when he recovered. When they reached Zanzibar, where Burton fell sick, Speke would not wait for him to recover, though Burton asked him to. Instead, he hurried home to England, where he began spreading lies about Burton and claiming all the credit for the expedition. Though he had promised Burton he would not speak before the Royal Geographical Society until he was with him, he began arrangements at once for another expedition, leaving his chief out in the cold. The Society, believing his stories about

Burton's incompetency and his cheating of his porters—an out-and-out lie—sent him in company with Captain Grant to visit Lake Victoria Nyanza. Even so, Speke failed to make a thorough exploration, which was not done until 1874, when Stanley circumnavigated it.

Burton was not to get a chance to defend himself for five years.

He applied to Lord Russell for a consular post. Russell replied that the best he could do was Fernando Po.[10] This best was the worst, for the post, known as the Foreign Office Grave, was a low hot fever-ridden island in the bight of Biafra, off West Africa. The very year Burton was to come there a yellow fever epidemic would kill off in two months seventy-eight out of two hundred and fifty white men. He would be paid the sum of seven hundred pounds a year for the chance of losing his life. This man whose knowledge of the East and whose abilities fitted him for the highest posts in India or Egypt, including the viceroyship, was given the lowest rung in the ladder of diplomatic service. Nevertheless, Burton, who had a new and young wife, had to have some sort of salary. And it was a step.

"They would like me to die," he said, "but I don't mean to."

As if that were not enough, the East India Company, whose army had now come under the Crown, took advantage of this chance to strike his name off their half-pay lists. The rule was that no Indian officer could take another appointment and keep his pay. It was generally ignored, but John Company wanted to get rid of their troublesome and too-outspoken Ruffian Dick. Off came his name, and he was left with no money at all.

When he first appeared at Nanny Po, he was watched curiously by everybody. The whites there had allowed the Negroes to gain the upper hand, partly because English law so protected the natives they could sue a white man for practically anything. British prestige was suffering; the natives were becoming arrogant.

A few days after Burton arrived, a large Black man, dressed

---

[10] An island off the west coast of Africa, now known as Bioko, and the northernmost part of Equatorial Guinea. The island was sometimes referred to as "Nanny Po."

like a dandy, walked into the consulate. He slapped Burton on the back, laughing loudly. "How do, Consul," he said, holding out his hand. "Come to shake hands—how do?"

Some Englishmen standing around watched Burton, for he would set the attitude of the whites for some time to come. Burton fixed upon the intruder his fierce glare, then shouted to his Kru boys to throw the uninvited guest out. Whooping with joy, his canoe boys leaped upon the big man and bodily tossed him out the window, which fortunately was only four feet from the groud. The cast-out one landed with a thud, got to his feet. and ran off. And there was no doubt from then on as to who was master in Fernando Po.

Nor was he soft with the whites who disputed with him. The rule was that every ship that stopped there should wait eighteen hours so that the merchants could have a chance to receive and answer their letters of business. Otherwise, so rare were boats, they might have to wait for a long time. But the captains had gotten into the custom of ignoring this and of sailing as soon as they had discharged their cargo. The first captain who tried that ran up against an iron wall. Burton pointed out that the delay was part of the ship's contract. The captain replied that none of the other consuls had tried to enforce the rule.

"Ha!" replied Richard. "More shame to them! Now, are you going to stay?"

"No, sir, not I."

"Very well then. I am going up to the Governor's, and I am going to load two cannons. If you go out *one minute* before your eighteen hours expires, I'll send the first shot across your bows and the second slap into you. I'm a man of my word. Good Morning!"

Stunned, the captain left, and he was so sure of Richard's word that he did not leave until half an hour after his time was up. And every other captain from then on made certain that he too stayed the lawful limit.

Meanwhile, Burton visited every place along the mainland coast, was the first man to scale the Pico Grands, the highest peaks of the Cameroon mountains, hunted gorillas, unsuccessfully, and investigated cannibalism. He reported that the Fang tribesmen, so famous for eating their prisoners of war, did not seem to have their hearts in it.

One of the places he wished to visit was the land of Dahomey. Lord Russell, hearing of this, appointed Burton as a commissioner. He was to protest to King Gelele against the great slave trade and also to ask that the Customs of the country be abandoned. The Customs in this case meant the slaughter of hundreds, perhaps thousands, of prisoners of war and of criminals. The land was a cruel and bloody one, where the king cut a man's throat every time he wanted to send a messenger to the ghosts of his dead ancestors. Animals were tied up in the most agonizing positions; the king had had pregnant women cut open while alive so that he might see what it was like.

And there was an army of Amazons there, genuine women-warriors.

Of course, the Foreign Office did their best to cripple his chances of success. Burton knew the king would only listen to a man who brought pleasing gifts. Yet the Foreign Office sent only a few, and these largely useless. And they did not send what the king had very much wanted; an English carriage and horses. Their feeble excuse was that the horses could not stand the climate. Burton swore, because it should have been left up to him to get the horses to Agbome, the capital, alive. But, handicapped as he was, he must go ahead and see what he could do.

Their progress was slow. Every half mile they had to stop to endure ceremonial dancing and drinking, given by every chief of a village, which often consisted only of a half a dozen huts. And every chief expected a gift.

But they did make up songs about him.

> "Batunu (Burton) he has seen the world with its kings and caboceers, He now comes to Dahomey, and he shall see everything here."

They halted finally at Kana, the king's winter quarters. Buko-no

Uro, Gelele's doctor and chief wizard, came to tell them that Gelele would receive them in the morning. Burton knew from bitter experience that the African liked to hurry up the white man, then to make him sit in the hot sun in full uniform for hours in front of a mud wall, and let him sweat until the potentate put in a leisurely appearance. So, though he was supposed to be at the so-called English house at ten A.M., he did not go until one in the afternoon. And then he was an hour early.

Here he met various dignitaries. One was Yevogan, the viceroy of Whydah. He was used to white men who cringed before him because of his power. He tried, jokingly, but really in earnest, to pull Burton and his companions off their stools. Under orders from the consul, they firmly resisted him. It would undoubtedly ruin their mission if they were to lose face at the very outset. Besides, Burton was not the kind to allow any man to unseat him. They reviewed a parade of warriors, then went to the palace.

They passed the king's sleeping room, which was paved with the skulls of neighboring princes, so that he might walk on them.

The king, Gelele, finally appeared. He was a tall man, well built, between forty and forty-five, his nails long as a Chinese mandarin's, his teeth blackened by tobacco. His eyes were red, bleared, inflamed. It was not bloodlust that caused this, but the glare of the sun during the long reception hours, the harsh winds, too much smoking, and too much time in bed with his many wives. Under the law, every woman in the country was his wife, and if one pleased his eye, he could take her. And often did. Nor could the husband protest, for he, like every man, was the king's legal slave.

There were women everywhere, unarmed women as well as the many Amazons. All notable for their intense devotion to His Majesty. If he sweated, they at once wiped off his brow; if he wished to spit, a royal wife offered him a gold spittoon; if he sneezed, everyone touched the ground with their heads; if he drank, all gave a blessing.

Burton saw at once that conversation was going to be tedious, for the king had to address the Meu, or chief general and tax gatherer, who spoke to the interpreter, who spoke to Burton. He determined to attack the language, which he did, and before he left Agbome, he could understand most conversations in Efon and could carry on a simple dialog.

Healths were drunk, but the king, after touching their glasses, had a white calico screen put up before him, so he could drink in privacy. At this, guns were fired, Amazons tinkled bells, ministers bent to the ground, clapping their hands, and the commoners, cowering to avoid the sight, turned their backs, if sitting, or danced, if standing, and made paddling motions with their hands.

Afterwards, salutes were fired. The first was for the king; then, eleven for Commodore Wilmot who had once made a mission to Gelele, and nine for the consul. Burton insisted that he be given the same number as his predecessor. Beecham, one of their native interpreters, turned blue with fear because of the consul's boldness in dealing with the savage monarch; nevertheless, he interpreted. The king at once apologized, saying it had been a mistake, and two more shots were fired. Then Burton's party retired.

The Amazons, Burton noted, were all big strapping women, so masculine they could usually be distinguished from the men only by their great buttocks. On the other hand, the men were somewhat effeminate. Even at that moment a party of warrior women were off attacking a village in the country of the Makhis, whose king had insulted Gelele.

This was truly a country of women, for they took precedence over men everywhere. Even the women slaves of the Amazons wore bells that warned men to get out of the way and not to dare to look at them. Burton had been very much annoyed on the way up to Agbome because his pace had been cut down to half a mile an hour, his men had been so busy throwing down their burdens and taking off for the bush at every tinkle.

A grand review was given in his honor. Past him filed in barbaric—and often ragged and dirty—splendor, battalions of full-breasted soldiery. The she-Mingan led the first brigade, flags and umbrellas on every side of her. After her came the she-Meu and the royal bodyguard, the Fanti, big-muscled women who danced as they marched and swung blades eighteen inches long, shaped exactly like a razor. These whistled through the air as the women demonstrated how they would cut off their enemies' heads. Behind them, the blunderbuss women, then the ammunition bearers; the elephant huntresses, musketeers, bow women, scouts, and stretcher bearers.

Men applauded but did not crowd close. It was high treason and death or exile even to touch an Amazon by accident. As the king's wives, they were vowed to chastity. Despite this, the king had just discovered that one hundred and fifty of his virgins were pregnant. Most of the men pointed out as guilty were punished, but most of the females were pardoned.

"After all," the king remarked to the consul, "women will be women."

After the review, the king stalked off, while men ran ahead of him, pointing out every stick and stone with finger-snappings and smoothing out every roughness so he might not stumble.

The English went to their unpleasant quarters, where they would be kept for two months while the endless talking and feasts of the African would go on. The Buko-no Uro came and asked to see the presents for the king. Burton refused, saying that the king himself must first see them. Burton then insisted strongly that if anybody were to be put to death in his presence, he would leave at once for Whydah and not come back.

Late in the morning Burton appeared with his gifts, passed through the Gate of Tears, and went on into the inner court. Here women sold provisions on one side, while on the other was dead King Gezo's huge war drum, hung with wreaths of skulls. Burton showed with a sinking heart the things that the Foreign Office had sent. Gelele reacted as he had expected; there was not even one word of thanks from the sullen king. The tent was far too small, and its pegs, instead of being of silver, were of wood, which would last not very long in this land of wood-eating insects. The heavy silver pipe was never used, Gelele preferring his lighter clay with the wood stem. The silver belts were also rejected, because Gelele had specifically asked for bracelets. Like all Africans, he took it as a personal slight if his wishes were not carried out to the letter. The coat of mail was too heavy and hot, so the king hung it up as a target to shoot at. Only the silver trays were admired, but the king had to ask what they were for.

"What about the carriages and the horses?" said Gelele, still looking around him as if he expected Burton to produce them from a hat.

Burton, concealing his exasperation, answered for the twelfth time that the Queen had feared that the horses might die and that it was very difficult to transport carriages.

"But carriages have been brought before," said Gelele, "and if the horses died even on the beach of Whydah, I would at least have known that the white Queen thought enough of Gelele to send them." He was very cold and haughty, but evidently seething inside.

Though he knew that now was not the time, Burton then asked if Gelele would do anything about stopping the slave trade and also abandoning or at least greatly reducing the slaughter and torture of prisoners.

Gelele did not reply.

Dismissed, Burton returned to his house, where his landlord, the old Buko-no, told him of his trouble with his latest wife, a young one. As he was married to eighty women, the Buko-no was having trouble in keeping them happy. Would Batunu have in his medicine bag a charm that would pep up the Buko-no? Burton replied that he was sorry but he did not. Not only was the old man disappointed, but his wives later heard of it and scolded him soundly for having asked for an aphrodisiac, as it reflected on their own stimulating abilities.

On St. John's Day, the war chiefs were seen coming in from out-stations and parading before the palace. Burton was sick at this news, for this meant the Customs would soon begin.

The rites were to supply the late father of Gelele with fresh attendants in ghostland. Some idea of how they were carried out could be told from the people's name for them, the *Khwe-ta-nun*, or Yearly Head Thing. It was not true, however, that the king paddled about a pool of human blood in a canoe. The two pits used to collect blood were only about two feet deep and four in diameter, not large enough for a boat.

Burton was stunned for days by the constant procession of soldiers, male and Amazon, the booming and barking of guns, the singing, the dancing, the drinking, the gaudy flashing display of colors and arms, the speeches, the drums forever beating. Once the king threw money into the crowd and in the frantic scramble men were killed and had eyes gouged out and noses bitten off. Even Burton and his party had to submit to scrambling for the cowrie shells which passed as currency, but the fight was strictly among themselves, with no bloodshed.

The king then walked up to the shed where the victims-to-be sat on stools. He threw cowrie shells among them, which were placed by attendants upon the prisoners' caps. Then Gelele snapped his fingers at Burton—the Dahomean version of the handshake—and the interpreter said that if Burton cared to plead, some of the victims might be pardoned.

This was not a way of making Burton lose face, but was part of the Customs formula, whereby the king might show his big heart. Burton replied that mercy well becomes great kings. So half of the prisoners were released, and heard their pardon while they crouched on all fours. Another speech; a clash of cymbals, a drinking of rum, and Burton's party was given permission to leave the royal presence.

The Evil Nights came, when no man except officials could stir outside without being beheaded. Burton chafed because he would get no chance to learn what really happened. On the other hand, he had himself told the king that he would not witness any executions. He believed that the victims were all made drunk with rum and that the king began by bringing his sharp blade down on the neck of a kneeling criminal. Afterwards, the high officials would also cut off heads.

He knew that every time the king thought a report should be sent to his father's ghost, he would charge a man or woman with a message and then send them off via the decapitation route. Such trivial things as making a new drum, being visited by a white man, or even moving from one place to another, required the services of another victim. He estimated that not less than five hundred were slaughtered at the yearly Customs, nor less than one thousand during the year of the Grand Customs, held when a king died. Whenever the king fell ill, many were also killed on suspicion of witchcraft.

It was plain to Burton that abolishing human sacrifice would be the same thing as abolishing Dahomey. The practice rose from the idea of honoring one's father and had been in long usage. The powerful priesthood supported it. Not only that, if the king did try to get rid of the Customs, he might end up being a sacrifice himself. Despite their groveling before the king, the captains and courtiers really held the power, and it was rumored that they had poisoned Gelele's grandfather because he had seemed to favor Christianity.

However, Burton noted this was the first time that no lives had been taken publicly, so he knew that his visit had driven the first small wedge into the eventual death of the Customs.

On the night of the fifth day, the deep boom of the death-drum and the firing of a musket told them that someone had died. In the morning, they rose to go to the palace. On their way they saw four corpses, dressed in white shirts and nightcaps, sitting on stools. Three men, naked, dangled head downwards from gallows. They had been beaten to death, and their genitals were cut off so as not to offend the king's wives with the sight.

Outside the Komasi house lay a dozen heads, face downwards. Within the palace gate were two more. At least twenty-three men had died during the Evil Night.

More parading, dancing and speeches followed. Burton sat through the late morning and most of the afternoon, making detailed notes about the barbaric spectacle. At last it came to an end, and Burton asked the king that he be allowed to rest the following day. Permission granted, he spent Sunday trying to drive out the noise from his ears and the dazzle and glitter from his eyes. All that day another phantom parade passed before him.

Burton watched the big Amazons carefully and noted that they were fiercer than the men. Part of this might be laid at their enforced continency, which he thought made them so irritable they wanted to fight. But the celibacy was hard to enforce; he noted that all the Passions are sisters, and that bloodshed caused these women to remember love, not to forget it. They were more savage than wounded gorillas, far more cruel than their brothers-in-arms.

However, their very existence was a drain upon the kingdom. The female troops, numbering twenty-five hundred, would produce about seventy-five hundred children. But they were forbidden issue, so that Dahomey, which had already lost many in their numerous wars, was fast sinking in population. Not only that, but Dahomey was constantly weakened by her export slave trade. She was no longer as feared by her neighbors as she had been, and the Egbas had twice repulsed Gelele with heavy losses. He was to try again to take Abeokuta, their capital, where his army would be crushed.

Monday, Burton passed through the city gate, where he saw the corpses, now being eaten by turkey-buzzards. Upon meeting Gelele, he was told that he ought to fight again for the cowries. Burton refused, as he wished to see how the king would take it. Besides, he had sprained a wrist in the last scramble. The king graciously excused him, then said that he must dance for him later on.

Burton had been putting off this honor, but the time came when he could no longer do so. One day the king announced that he must, so the consul gave the right timing to the band, then threw himself headlong into a violent Hindustani single step. Loud cheers, even from the king. Burton danced again. More cheers. Firing of guns and presenting of arms. Burton was a big success, and he was made an honorary brigadier-general of the Amazons.

The days and nights went on, with the king putting off the official reading of the message from Lord Russell. The drums beat, and the cymbals clashed to hide the cries of the victims, and every morning there would be fresh bodies for him to see, while the buzzards waited on nearby calabash trees. And for every male corpse displayed, Burton knew, there was a female to match it within the palace walls, where the women were slain.

Burton had spent six weeks in Agbome, and now he received word that a cruiser was waiting off of Whydah to take him to the Oil Rivers region. It could not stay too long, so he must get his business over, one way or the other. He ordered his bags to be openly packed in the house's compound, knowing that word of this would reach the king. He also sent two men to tell Gelele that the thirty porters he had asked for had not been delivered, and that he was setting out the next day, regardless.

The king flew into a rage because his ministers had neglected to deliver the porters, and had his Amazons drive them out of the palace with blows from bamboo sticks. Then the king sent an apology to Burton, saying that he could not at once attend to the consul's affairs because he was too angry. Two days later, the Customs came to an end. Typically violent, they finished with a wild drunken feast and the breaking of all the glass and the smashing of the furniture.

Two days later the king condescended to receive them to hear the message. "I hear that you have been complaining about me, O Batunu, and this after we have been the best of friends, dancing and drinking together."

"I have no grievance against you," replied Burton cautiously, "but it has not been well to hold up for two months such an important message."

"I have been busy," said Gelele. "Besides, you have already told me the substance of your message."

Burton then complained of having been kept practically a prisoner for two months in his house, that the Buko-no had subjected them to many small annoyances, and that they had been kept from hunting in the Makhi mountains to the north. The king passed these off with evasive answers. Burton became heated, and asked Gelele if he knew that they had been kept that afternoon for hours in the sun before the gate, a custom not followed in civilized countries. The king said he had not; then, to get off a disagreeable subject, joked with Burton about his having kept the house slaves in order with a light beating. Burton's frown disappeared; whereupon the king asked him to read his message.

Burton knew enough about the language by now to know if the interpreter was translating correctly, so he checked him. He suspected that during the first days of his visit his words had changed somewhat when going through the middle man. The interpreter had not cared to offend his king, for he might be exiled or even killed. Now, however, he told Gelele in straightforward words that the British government intended to put a stop to the slave traffic and that the United States would no longer let her ships carry slaves. As for the sacrifices, the less of them, the better Her Majesty's men would feel.

Burton felt hopeless, for it was evident from the king's face that he might as well be talking to the wind.

"The ruler of England and I are like my finger," said Gelele, "but your men-of-war are now capturing slavers near my beaches, and I cannot allow that."

Burton explained that in civilized countries the right of a nation extended no farther than three miles off shore, and the English ships had not come inside that. As for the king's excuses for not being able to end the Customs, the people would always follow the example of their ruler. Moreover, unless the spectacle of nude and mutilated corpses left to hang in the sun were spared visitors, Burton would advise all Englishmen to avoid the court during the time of the Customs.

Never before had anybody dared to speak up to the king in such a blunt fashion. He scowled, and his ministers shifted uneasily, perhaps wondering if they would have to call in the Amazons with their beheading knives.

Burton was in a tight spot, but he did not betray a lack of confidence. Gelele, of course, had no real idea of what Great Britain was; he thought of it as a slightly larger and richer Dahomey, surrounded by water and inhabited by white men. Nevertheless, if he were calm, he would never consider going to war with England. He was having enough trouble with his war against the Egbas.

But he was a totally arrogant man whose slightest wish was instantly carried out, and he did not like being rebuked before his ministers and wives. A moment's anger, and he might give the order that would send his savage women to drag Burton off. Also, there was always the temptation of the glory the king would have if he owned the skull of the great Batunu for his drinking cup. No other West Coast monarch could boast such a splendid possession.

Gelele's bloodshot eyes gleamed, while Burton waited for his reply. Then, slowly, a smile replaced the scowl, and the consul breathed easier.

There was more talk. Nothing came of it, except that Burton knew he would have to report that there was little Her Majesty's government could do about the slave trade or the sacrifices except to allow them to die out. At eight p.m. the king said he was tired of talking.

"If you are not still angry, Batunu, we will drink together."

Burton diplomatically replied that he had never felt personally displeased with Gelele, just with his ministers, who had given him a hard time. They stood up and drank gin. No noise was made at this time; the ministers, not wishing to draw the king's attention to them, were happy just to kiss the ground as he left. At the doorway which was too narrow for two abreast, Burton fell back. The king asked why he had done that. Burton said that crowned heads always walked first. Pleased, Gelele shook hands with him.

"You are a good man but," he added, rolling his head, "you are too angry."

Nor would Burton promise to come back for another visit. Though the king might pardon him this time for his anger because of the novelty, the next incident might find him in a less pleasant mood. And there would be no restraining the famous Burton temper, if he were pushed too far.

He went back to Fernando Po, where he was granted a leave to England. Lord Russell wrote to thank him, saying he had carried out the mission to his "entire satisfaction." This was in a personal note to Mrs. Burton, however. As usual, Burton received no official recommendation.

On his return from Dahomey, Burton found that Speke and Grant had come back from their central African expedition and were receiving a tremendous ovation. Despite the injuries done him, Burton was the first to praise his work. Then, on hearing Speke's account, he changed his mind, for it was apparent to him that the two had spent much time in accomplishing little, that their story was full of errors. Others found this out; Speke's reputation fell as Burton's rose. And he could take pride in the fact that it was his labor that had made the road easy for them. He had opened the way for Englishmen; they had only to follow him.

Burton challenged his former friend to discuss the sources of the Nile with him before the Royal Society at Bath. Speke agreed. At the same time, Burton was told that Speke had said that if Burton appeared at Bath, Speke would kick him.

"Well, that settles it!" roared Burton. "By God, he shall kick me!"

When the day came for the debate, excitement had reached a high pitch all over England. Ruffian Dick was boiling mad, so went the rumor, and anything could happen. Though broken in health by his travels and no longer a young man, he could challenge Speke to a secret duel. If so, the money would be on him. People still remembered his exhibition duel with a French hussar in which he had struck the man's saber so hard he'd knocked it out of his hand seven times in a row. And the Frenchman had had to beg off, saying his arm was numbed by the terrific force.

The first day there was to be no discussion about Africa, but the two sat on the same platform. Speke looked at Burton, then at Mrs. Burton, who had talked to him in an effort at reconciliation. His face was sad and yearning and perplexed. Then it hardened. As the speeches went on, he began to fidget. Presently, he rose, muttering, "Oh, I cannot stand this any longer." Burton remained.

The next day, a larger crowd than ever assembled. Burton and his wife stood on the platform, alone. His notes were in his hand, held like a pistol ready to fire. But Speke did not appear, and they waited in a gathering tension for twenty-five minutes. Suddenly, the council and the speakers filed in. The president arose and announced that Speke had been shot while hunting that morning. His friends had heard the gun and seen him stagger. Running up, they had found him wounded, close to the heart. Within a few minutes, he was dead.

Burton sank into his chair, his face pale and working. Called on to speak, he talked briefly of other matters. When he got home, he wept long and hard, and Mrs. Burton spent days trying to soften his grief.

Whether Speke had been the victim of an accident, or whether he committed suicide because he could not face the man about whom he had lied, was never known. The jury said that it was accidental death.

Unable to kill him off at Fernando Po, the Ministry now gave him the consulship at Santos, Brazil. Though not as unhealthy as his first post, it was not far behind. However, it was a step up the ladder, and he beat the heat, fever, and plague as he had done in Africa, by establishing residence at a place high in the hills, further inland. He traveled much, hunted for diamonds and sea serpents, and finally, while home on sick leave, was appointed to the consulship of Damascus. Both of the posts were gotten through the efforts of his wife. During her lifetime she wrote, literally, thousands of letters to the high statesmen, pointing out that they were ignoring her Richard's great talents and accomplishments in favor of lesser men. She cornered officials and drove them to desperation with her praises of her husband. However, Lord Derby, held a high opinion of Richard and was pleased to get him Damascus, a high post.

No less joyed were the Burtons, for he would be home once again in his beloved East. But there he ran afoul of a combination of several cliques. One was represented by the Turkish governor of Syria, a fat and, corrupt beast. Another was his jealous superior, the consul-general at Beirout. A third, the Christian missionaries, who resented Burton's free thinking philosophy and his close connections with Mohammedanism. A fourth were the Greek Orthodox. And a fifth were the Jewish money-lenders.

Burton narrowly prevented a wholesale slaughter of Christians by Muslims aroused by the too-ardent preaching of a British missionary. He browbeat the Turkish governor into sending his Muslim soldiers out to stop the riot. But the consul-general wrote home that the danger was imaginary. The missionary who had been saved a martyr's death wrote letters home, accusing Burton of hostility to Christians. Rashid Pasha, the governor of Syria, laid an ambush for Burton with three hundred Bedawins.[11] Isabel found out about it and warned him so that he slipped away. But she got him into trouble herself by getting him to protect the Shazli sect, which was thinking about wholesale conversion to Roman Catholicism. Rashid warned Burton that he was taking onto himself too much authority. Burton had many Jews as friends but the Damascus money-lenders were not among them. It was a fact that they were charging many poor peasants interest even higher than sixty percent; the natives who fell into their clutches could not get out of them. Burton could not stop the practices, but he did refuse to help the money-lenders collect their debts. Offended, these wrote to the wealthy and influential Jews in England, claiming to represent "all the Jews of Damascus" and complaining falsely of persecution. The English Jews, of course, had no way of checking up on the stories. He earned more hate from Rashid because he warned the Druze Arabs that the Turk was trying to use them as a cat's paw by stirring up revolt among them.

While visiting Nazareth, Isabel Burton had a thieving Copt thrown out of her tent. He threw stones at her servants; they beat him. Just then, a crowd of Greeks came out of a church close by. They hated Burton because he had defended the Jews when they had protested against the Turks selling a synagogue of theirs to the Greek bishop. Now they seized their chance and stoned Burton and his party. Many struck him; one hurt his sword arm so badly he was crippled for two years afterwards. He stood his ground, calmly picking out the ringleaders among the raving mob of one hundred and fifty. But when three of his servants were badly hurt,

---

[11] Burton himself said: "I was never more flattered in my life, than to think it would take three hundred men to kill me."

he grabbed a revolver from the belt of a man and shot over the heads of the crowd. Isabel ran off for help, and ten Americans and Germans, armed, came running. The mob fled in panic.

The storm of wrath broke, Burton with his self-defeating sense of timing, delayed sending the report on the incident. Meanwhile, every party and sect he had offended, forgetting the many good things he had done for them, clamored for his recall. A cool investigation on the part of the government would have disclosed their consul's innocence of the charges made against him. But, fearing to offend Turkey, the Foreign Office listened to the flood of complaints. One day, as Burton was getting ready for one of his long rides into the desert, he was handed a note. It had been sent by his successor, the first notice he had of what had happened.

Too proud to appeal, he left at once. But he had the satisfaction of seeing hundreds of the people gather in a popular demonstration of their love and respect for him. Later, Rashid and the Greek bishop would be disgraced, and the ringleaders of the money-lenders would go bankrupt.

His friends at home came to his rescue too late. The best they could get him was the third rate consulship at Trieste. He could not afford to refuse it as he still clung to the hope that someday he would get the post at Morocco. Isabel kept up her agitation for him, but Lord Salisbury put her off. Even so, he might have gotten Morocco had not Salisbury's party gone out of power.

For thirty years he had been thinking of making a translation of the *One Thousand and One Nights*, better known as the *Arabian Nights*. He knew well this great collection of fairy stories, for in his disguises he had often entertained the crowds in the marketplace and coffee shops with them. Now he set himself to his task, one for which he was fitted better than anybody else in the world. Not especially inspired as a prose writer or a poet, he was a magnificent interpreter. Not only that, but he refused to issue a castrated version. Mrs. Grundy[12] could go to hell if she

---

[12] Mrs. Grundy originated as an unseen character in Thomas Morton's 1798 play *Speed the Plough* and is a figurative name for an extremely conventional or priggish person.

objected to the many spicy tales and utterly frank language of the characters. What was dirty in England was not necessarily so in the mouths of Ali Baba and Aladdin and the naughty ladies kept under lock and key by the genies. Another attraction were his many footnotes, containing vast knowledge of Eastern lore, including many curious bits of sexology. His readers ate up the first issue and clamored for more. He pocketed twelve thousand pounds and calmly accepted alike the bitter denunciations of outraged prudes and the compliments of scholars and statesmen. "Now I know the tastes of England," he said to Isabel, "we never need be without money."

But what his explorations had not done, his pen had. One day there came a telegram addressed to Sir Richard Burton. Thinking is a practical joke, Burton refused it at first, but when he opened it, found that Queen Victoria had made him a Knight Commander of St. Michael and St. George. It was not the wished-for K.C.B., the Knights Commander of the Order of the Bath, but it was enough of an honor to make him happy for some time and to send his wife into an ecstasy.

The thrill passed. An Irish-American journalist, Frank Harris, visiting Burton at Trieste, called him a desert lion dying in the cage. He was dying of disappointment and boredom and lack of outlet for his great abilities. In spite of literary talents and great gift of speech, he was fundamentally a man of action, a leader.

Harris, who worshipped Burton, asked if he would have preferred to be viceroy of India or consul-general of Egypt.

"Egypt! Egypt!" cried the old man. "In India I should have had the English civil servants to deal with—Jangali, or savages, as their Hindu fellow-subjects call them—and English prejudices, formalities, stupidity, ignorance. They would have killed me in India, thwarted me, intrigued against me, murdered me. But in Egypt I could have made my own civil servants, trained them. I could have had natives, too, to help. Ah, what a chance!

". . . I know the Arab nature. The Mahdi business could have been settled without a blow," he exploded, speaking of the revolt that had killed his friend, "Chinese" Gordon. "What did

Dufferin[13] know of Egypt? Poor Dufferin, what did he even know of Dufferin?"

He told how he had come back from Africa and offered all East Africa to Lord Salisbury. He'd made treaties with all the chiefs, and no other nation was interested enough to object. But Salisbury asked if East Africa was worth anything. Twenty years afterwards, the Germans had moved in to take over colonies which England was to buy with blood during the First World War.

He ended up, "England . . . makes me an office-boy."

So he finished his days at Trieste, literally eating himself into the grave. Gout and gas around the heart, brought on by the tremendous appetite of the disappointed, steadily crippled him. He grew too weak to handle the iron cane that he always carried to keep his sword arm strong. The night of the 19th of October, 1891 as Isabel was saying her night prayers to him, a dog howled. Richard took that as an omen of death, as he had done the tapping of a bird at his window three days before. He went to bed, became sick at midnight, and at four in the morning, crying out, "Oh, Puss—chloroform—ether—or I am a dead man!" he died in his wife's arms.

At his funeral at Trieste, the entire population of one hundred and fifty thousand turned out to say farewell to the beloved consul. His body was then shipped to Mortlake, in England, where he was buried in a tomb built in the form of the Arabian tent he had loved so well.

Justin Huntley McCarthy and Swinburne wrote poems about him, but the finest tribute is undoubtedly that given by Walter Phelps Dodge in his book on Burton.

"Who can doubt that he faced the crossing of the Styx with the same coolness and courage he had ever shown! or that his hail of Charon bore the right accent!"

---

[13] **Frederick Temple Hamilton-Temple-Blackwood, 1st Marquess of Dufferin and Ava** (1826-1902) was a British public servant and prominent member of Victorian society. In 1882 Dufferin travelled to Egypt as British commissioner and wrote a report (known as the Dufferin Report) detailing how the occupation was to benefit Egypt, with plans for development which were to progressively re-involve Egyptians in running the country.

About the Authors

Philip José Farmer was born on January 26, 1918 in North Terre Haute, Indiana. He grew up in Peoria, Illinois where he spent much of his childhood reading everything from the Bible and books on mythology to the classics by Baum, Carroll, Cervantes, Defoe, Dickens, Homer, London, Swift, and Twain to popular works by Burroughs, Doyle, Haggard, Verne, and Wells.

He sold his first story, a mainstream tale titled "O'Brien and Obrenov," to *Adventure* in 1946 before he decided to try his hand at science fiction. His next published story, "The Lovers," appeared in the August 1952 issue of *Startling Stories*, and is noted for breaking the taboo on sex in science fiction, as well as for earning Farmer a Hugo Award for "Most Promising New Talent."

Married and with two children, he soon quit his job to become a full-time writer, but after selling several more stories to the science fiction pulps, his career hit a stumbling block when he "won" the Shasta Prize Novel Contest. The grand prize was four thousand dollars (a lot of money in 1953), but he never received his winnings. Instead, the publisher asked Farmer for rewrites while the prize money was invested in another book, which bombed. By the time the truth came out, Farmer had lost his house and was forced to take up full time employment.

Farmer left Peoria with his family in 1956 and moved around the country working as a technical writer for the space-defense industry, eventually ending up in Beverly Hills, California in 1965. All the while he continued to write and sell science fiction short stories and novels, launching his popular World of Tiers series and even winning a second Hugo Award for the novella "Riders of the Purple Wage." Then, just before the moon landing in 1969, he was laid off from his technical writing job, so he decided to write fiction full time once again. This time it stuck.

In 1970, Farmer moved back to Peoria with his family and again his career began to take off, this time with a third Hugo Award win, for *To Your Scattered Bodies Go*, the opening novel in his bestselling Riverworld series. For the next few years Farmer sought inspiration from the popular literature he so loved, writing novels such as *The Mad Goblin* (a Doc Savage pastiche), *Lord of the Trees* and *Lord Tyger* (both Tarzan pastiches), *The Wind Whales of Ishmael* (a science fiction sequel to *Moby Dick*), *The Other Log of Phileas Fogg* (the "true" story behind Jules Verne's *Around the World in Eighty Days*), and *Venus on the Half-Shell* (written as if by Kilgore Trout, a character from the works of Kurt Vonnegut). He also wrote two "biographies" during this period: *Tarzan Alive: A Definitive Biography of Lord Greystoke* and *Doc Savage: His Apocalyptic Life*.

The next two decades saw the publication of the Dayworld trilogy, as well as further installments in the Riverworld and World of Tiers series. Farmer also fulfilled his lifelong ambition to write an Oz novel, and authorized Doc Savage and Tarzan novels, with the publication of *A Barnstormer in Oz*, *Escape from Loki*, and *Tarzan and the Dark Heart of Time*. Late in his career, Farmer tried his hand at a different genre with *Nothing Burns in Hell*, a detective novel set in his hometown of Peoria.

After Farmer retired from writing in 1999, new collections such as *Pearls from Peoria* and *Venus on the Half-Shell and Others* continued to appear, as did new collaborative works such as *The Evil in Pemberley House* (with Win Scott Eckert), *The Song of Kwasin* (with Christopher Paul Carey), and *Dayworld: A Hole in Wednesday* (with Danny Adams).

Farmer passed on February 25, 2009, but his fan base is as ardent as ever, still gathering at anual FarmerCons.

Michael (Mick) Walton first came into contact with Sir Richard Burton when, in the early 1960s, class 2C of High Storrs Grammar School for Boys in Sheffield put in thrupence each so someone's elder brother could buy them a copy of *The Kama Sutra*, and although at the time he didn't quite know what a yoni was or exactly where to find it, it was clearly very, very important. (The book was also unpleasantly sticky by the time Mick read it, because Stephen Woodhead had got hold of it first.)

Flash forward fifteen years to the flea market in Vienna where he bought an English-language copy of Baedeker's 1883 *Guide to Southern Germany and Austria* which told the traveler that in Austro-Hungarian Trieste: "British Consul, Capt. Richard Burton, Piazza Barbacan (office hours 9.30-12.30 and 2-4.30)."

Then, some twenty years ago, he was given his first contract by the University of Trieste to teach English, which gave him the opportunity to research a "Burton Trail" of places connected to Sir Richard Burton in the city where he had spent the last eighteen years of his life, and which was published by the Trieste Civic Library.

Mick has also co-organized several exhibitions about Sir Richard Francis Burton in Trieste, established a series of conferences about him (Trieste 2015, Opatija 2017, Boulogne-sur-mer 2019, Torquay 2021, Tunis 2022) and published his own *Sir Richard Burton and His Circle* based around caricatures from the original *Vanity Fair*.

He lives in Italy with his partner, Carolyn—a Country Dance teacher (Honkey-Tonk Style)—and has supported Sheffield United through thick and thin (quite a lot of thin) for over sixty years.

Mark Hodder is an English author based in Valencia, Spain. His six-part series of Burton & Swinburne novels opened with *The Strange Affair of Spring-Heeled Jack*, which went on to win the 2010 Philip K. Dick Award. The following two novels, *The Curious Case of the Clockwork-Man* and *Expedition to the Mountains of the Moon*, were released in 2011 and 2012 respectively to wide acclaim, with the latter nominated for a Sidewise Award. His fourth novel in the Burton & Swinburne series, *The Secret of Abdu El Yezdi*, was also nominated for a Sidewise Award. Mark created and maintains BLAKIANA, a website dedicated to the fictional detective Sexton Blake. His novel *The Silent Thunder Caper* was the first Blake story to be officially sanctioned since 1978. Mark has recently edited new anthologies of Blake material and is currently working on an SF novel.

Paul Spiteri has published four short stories. The first, "Getting Ready to Write," was in collaboration with Philip José Farmer and was published in *Farmerphile* #13 (July 2008), and reprinted in *The Philip José Farmer Centennial Collection* (2018). He has also written several essays and book introductions related to Farmer. He was the editor of *Pearls from Peoria* (2006), a massive collection of Farmer rarities. With some version of retirement now in play he expects to devote more time to writing, and having a less unkempt garden!

He lives in Surrey, England where he may well house the largest Farmer collection in the UK. He shares his home with his darling wife, Claire, and awesome daughters Gina and Maddie. The family recently adopted two (male) cats, thus finally evening up the household gender balance.

Meteor House Titles

THE WORLDS OF PHILIP JOSÉ FARMER
Anthology Series edited by Michael Croteau
Volume 1: Protean Dimensions
Volume 2: Of Dust and Soul
Volume 3: Portraits of a Trickster
Volume 4: Voyages to Strange Days

The Best of Farmerphile edited by Michael Croteau
The Philip José Farmer Centennial Collection edited by Michael Croteau
Greatheart Silver and Other Pulp Heroes by Philip José Farmer
Up from the Bottomless Pit by Philip José Farmer

WOLD NEWTON SERIES
Doc Savage: His Apocalyptic Life by Philip José Farmer
Tarzan and the Dark Heart of Time by Philip José Farmer

THE KHOKARSA SERIES
Exiles of Kho by Christopher Paul Carey
Flight to Opar (Restored Edition) by Philip José Farmer
The Song of Kwasin by Philip José Farmer and Christopher Paul Carey
Hadon, King of Opar by Christopher Paul Carey
Blood of Ancient Opar by Christopher Paul Carey

THE PAT WILDMAN SERIES
The Evil in Pemberley House by Philip José Farmer and Win Scott Eckert
The Scarlet Jaguar by Win Scott Eckert

THE PHILEAS FOGG SERIES
Phileas Fogg and the War of Shadows by Josh Reynolds
Phileas Fogg and the Heart of Osra by Josh Reynolds

THE TWO HAWKS SERIES
Man of War by Heidi Ruby Miller

THE DAYWORLD SERIES
Dayworld: A Hole in Wednesday by Philip José Farmer and Danny Adams

SCIENCE FICTION ADVENTURE
The Abnormalities of Stringent Strange by Rhys Hughes
Airship Hunters by Jim Beard and Duane Spurlock

REFERENCE - CROSSOVERS
Crossovers Expanded, Volume 1 by Sean Lee Levin
Crossovers Expanded, Volume 2 by Sean Lee Levin

CHAPBOOKS
*Being an Account of the Delay at Green River, Wyoming, of Phileas Fogg,
World Traveler, or, The Masked Man Meets an English Gentleman*
by Win Scott Eckert
*The Adventure of the Fallen Stone: Being the First Part of the Account of
The Dynamics of a Meteor* by John H. Watson, M.D.
edited by Win Scott Eckert
Watch Your Back, Mr. Minamoto by Frank Schildiner

Visit us at meteorhousepress.com